Single-Session Integrated CBT

In this book, Windy Dryden takes long-standing research on single-session integrated therapy and transfers it to the field of CBT in a timely and conceptual application.

This thoroughly updated new edition offers brand new chapters on single-session thinking. The book questions the common practice of predicating therapist training on the notion that therapy is an ongoing process. Based on his extensive work demonstrating the benefits of single-session CBT to public and professional audiences, Dryden has developed a single-session approach for work in the therapy and coaching fields. Comprising 30 key points, and divided into two parts – Theory and Practice – it concisely covers the key features of SSI-CBT.

This book offers essential guidance for students and practitioners experienced in CBT, as well as practitioners from other theoretical orientations who require an accessible guide to the distinctive theoretical and practical features of this exciting new approach.

Windy Dryden, PhD, is Emeritus Professor of Psychotherapeutic Studies at Goldsmiths, University of London. He is an international authority on Rational Emotive Behaviour Therapy and is in part-time clinical and consultative practice. He has worked in psychotherapy for more than 45 years and is the author and editor of over 250 books.

T0299791

CBT Distinctive Features
Series Editor: Windy Dryden

Cognitive behaviour therapy (CBT) occupies a central position in the move towards evidence-based practice and is frequently used in the clinical environment. Yet there is no one universal approach to CBT and clinicians speak of first, second and even third wave approaches.

This series provides straightforward, accessible guides to a number of CBT methods, clarifying the distinctive features of each approach. The series editor, Windy Dryden, successfully brings together experts from each discipline to summarise the 30 main aspects of their approach, divided into theoretical and practical features.

The CBT Distinctive Features Series will be essential reading for psychotherapists, counsellors, and psychologists of all orientations who want to learn more about the range of new and developing cognitive behaviour approaches.

Recent titles in the series:

Single-Session Integrated CBT: Distinctive Features 2nd Edition by Windy Dryden

Beck's Cognitive Therapy: Distinctive Features 2nd Edition by Frank Wills

Rational Emotive Behaviour Therapy: Distinctive Features 3rd Edition by Windy Dryden

Integrating CBT and 'Third Wave' Therapies by Dr Fiona Kennedy and Dr David Pearson

Motivational Cognitive Behavioural Therapy by Cathy Atkinson, Paul Earnshaw

Cognitive Behavioural Chairwork by Matthew Pugh

Emotional Schema Therapy by Robert L. Leahy

Mindfulness-Based Cognitive Therapy 2nd Edition by Rebecca Crane

For further information about this series please visit www.routledge.com/CBT-Distinctive-Features/book-series/DFS

Single-Session Integrated CBT

Distinctive Features

2nd Edition

Windy Dryden

Routledge
Taylor & Francis Group

LONDON AND NEW YORK

Second edition published 2022
by Routledge
2 Park Square, Milton Park, Abingdon, Oxon, OX14 4RN

and by Routledge
605 Third Avenue, New York, NY 10158

Routledge is an imprint of the Taylor & Francis Group, an informa business

First edition published by Routledge 2016

British Library Cataloguing-in-Publication Data
A catalogue record for this book is available from the British Library

Library of Congress Cataloging-in-Publication Data
Names: Dryden, Windy, author.
Title: Single-session integrated CBT: distinctive features / Windy Dryden.
Description: Second edition. | Milton Park, Abingdon, Oxon; New York, NY: Routledge, 2022. | Series: CBT distinctive features | Includes bibliographical references and index.
Identifiers: LCCN 2021037546 (print) | LCCN 2021037547 (ebook) | ISBN 9781032102788 (hardback) | ISBN 9781032102771 (paperback) | ISBN 9781003214557 (ebook)
Subjects: LCSH: Cognitive therapy.
Classification: LCC RC489.C63 D796 2022 (print) | LCC RC489.C63 (ebook) | DDC 616.89/1425–dc23
LC record available at https://lccn.loc.gov/2021037546
LC ebook record available at https://lccn.loc.gov/2021037547

ISBN: 9781032102788 (hbk)
ISBN: 9781032102771 (pbk)
ISBN: 9781003214557 (ebk)

DOI: 10.4324/9781003214557

Typeset in Times New Roman
by Newgen Publishing UK

Contents

Introduction   1

Part I THEORY   **9**

1   Single-Session Integrated CBT (SSI-CBT): what it is and some basic assumptions   11

2   The single-session mindset in SSI-CBT   20

3   Working alliance theory: A generic framework for SSI-CBT   30

4   People largely create and maintain their problems by a range of cognitive-behavioural factors   37

5   As far as possible, clients should be helped to deal healthily with the adversity involved in their problem, whether real or inferred   42

6   Human beings have the capability to help themselves quickly under specific circumstances   50

7   It is important to privilege your clients' viewpoints in SSI-CBT   54

8   Dealing with the suitability issue   58

9   A focus on problems, goals and solutions is important in SSI-CBT   64

10   Carry out a full assessment of the client's nominated problem drawing on case formulation principles   73

11 In SSI-CBT, it is possible to help clients identify and deal with a central mechanism responsible for the existence of their problems   78
12 The client's subsequent responses to their first reaction are often more important than the first reaction itself   84
13 It is important to draw upon a range of client variables in SSI-CBT   90
14 Helpful client characteristics for SSI-CBT   95
15 Helpful therapist characteristics for SSI-CBT   102

Part II PRACTICE   **109**
16 Good practice in SSI-CBT   111
17 An overview of the SSI-CBT process   123
18 The first contact   127
19 Pre-session preparation   131
20 The session, 1: Beginning well   136
21 The session, 2: Creating a focus   140
22 The session, 3: Understanding the nominated problem   147
23 The session, 4: Setting a goal   156
24 The session, 5: Identifying the central mechanism   169
25 The session, 6: Dealing with the central mechanism   176
26 The session, 7: Making an impact   184
27 The session, 8: Encouraging the client to apply learning inside and outside the session   193
28 The session, 9: Ending well   198
29 After the session: Reflection, the recording and the transcript   202
30 Follow-up and evaluation   204

References   211
Index   217

Introduction

In this introduction, I place single-session therapy (SST) in its recent historical context and outline why I became interested in this way of working that culminated in me developing what I call Single-Session Integrated Cognitive Behaviour Therapy (SSI-CBT).

Single-session therapy: some recent history

This book adds to the growing literature on single-session therapy (SST) that has blossomed since Moshe Talmon's (1990) seminal book on the subject. Three recent conferences on single-session work and walk-in clinics (where a lot of this work takes place) have been held, twice in Australia (2012 and 2019) and once in Canada (2015). This attests to the international interest that this way of working has attracted (see Hoyt, Bobele, Slive, Young & Talmon, 2018; Hoyt & Talmon, 2014a; Hoyt, Young & Rycroft, 2021).

Until recently, therapist training was based on the idea that therapy is an ongoing process and that clients attending for only one or two sessions were considered 'dropouts' from the process. People in the SST field have consistently questioned this notion. Talmon (1990), for example, reported on informal retrospective research that he carried out on 200 of his patients who attended only one session. He found that 78 per cent of this group said that they had got what they wanted from attending therapy, and only 10 per cent said that they did not like the therapist or the outcome of therapy. Following on from that, Hoyt, Talmon and Rosenbaum (1990) carried out a prospective study on planned single-session therapy with 60 clients, 58 of whom were reached on follow-up. Of

DOI: 10.4324/9781003214557-1

that final sample of 58, 34 did not require further therapy, 88 per cent reported 'much improvement' or 'improvement', and 79 per cent thought that SST was sufficient for them. This work suggested that the idea that people only attending for a single session of therapy can be considered 'dropouts' could be challenged. I, somewhat tongue-in-cheek, offered a new definition of 'dropouts' from therapy: 'A dropout from therapy is someone leaving therapy before their therapist believes they should.' Once it was accepted that productive work could be achieved in a single session, many people began to explore the idea of designing SST, leading to different developments depending upon therapeutic setting and orientation.

Concerning therapeutic setting, much SST occurs in walk-in services (sometimes known as drop-in centres),[1] as mentioned earlier. These are used mainly by people who want to talk when they need to and don't want to be burdened by using ongoing services. Although some of these clients do return, workers in these services assume that the session will be the only one they will have with the client and design the work accordingly. In another therapeutic setting, demonstrations of therapy in front of a live or online audience, or captured on DVD, are essentially single sessions as both therapist and client know that they will not meet again. It is my view that much productive work can be done in these sessions, and the work done in such demonstrations can usefully inform more formal SST (Dryden, 2018, 2019, 2021a, 2021b).

Regarding therapeutic orientation, it is perhaps no surprise that SST would appeal to theorists and practitioners of solution-focused therapy (SFT) with its emphasis on building solutions and utilising clients' strengths rather than on problem-solving and addressing clients' deficits. However, a wide variety of other therapeutic approaches have shown an interest in SST, including CBT. From a CBT perspective, Öst developed an effective single-session approach to treating various simple phobias (see Davis III, Ollendick & Öst, 2012), which is predicated on the idea that the patient needs to stay in the phobic situation until their levels of anxiety drop markedly. This necessitated that the single session often lasted significantly longer than the 50-minute therapeutic hour. As can be seen, this approach, while cognitive-behavioural in nature, very much relied on the patient's direct experience of the phobic object. This emphasis on experience is very much a feature of another CBT single-session treatment approach pioneered by Angela Reinecke (e.g. Reinecke, Waldenmaier, Cooper & Harmer, 2013) who modified a standard panic disorder treatment protocol (see Salkovskis, Clark, Hackmann, Wells & Gelder, 1999). After explaining the CBT model of panic disorder and the role of safety-seeking behaviour, and the importance of exposure to the feared situation without such behaviour, patients were given an immediate opportunity to practise this in a relevant situation. Very promising results have emerged from this single-session treatment. This emphasis on rehearsing the solution in the session is a hallmark of single-session work (Dryden, 2021c).

Single-session therapy: a personal journey

My interest in developing Single-Session Integrated Cognitive Behaviour Therapy (SSI-CBT) emerged from many sources. Like many counsellors trained in the 1970s, it was almost obligatory to watch the 'Gloria' films. Here, a client, Gloria, was interviewed by three therapists demonstrating their approach to therapy. What was remarkable about this series of films was that each of the therapists was the founder of the therapy approach being demonstrated: Carl Rogers (the founder of what is now known as Person Centred Therapy), Fritz Perl (the founder of Gestalt Therapy) and Albert Ellis (the founder of what is now known as Rational Emotive Behaviour Therapy).

Although not apparent at the time, these interviews were essentially examples of single-session therapy since Gloria did not have any more sessions with any of the therapists.[2] There were two further series of such films with clients known as 'Kathy' and 'Richard', which, while not having the same impact on the field that the Gloria films had, did show me what could be achieved in a single session by representatives of different cognitive-behavioural approaches. Thus, Arnold Lazarus (the founder of Multimodal Therapy, an approach rooted in CBT), Aaron T. Beck (the founder of Cognitive Therapy) and Donald Meichenbaum (a leading proponent of Cognitive Behaviour Modification) all worked effectively in the single session that they had with their respective clients.

Another significant influence on my interest in single-session work was the live sessions carried out by Albert Ellis at his famous Friday Night Workshops.[3] At these workshops, carried out every Friday evening when Albert Ellis was in town at his Institute in New York, Ellis interviewed two people on a particular emotional problem. After each interview, Ellis and the volunteer answered questions from members of the audience, who would often make pertinent observations.[4] Research done by Ellis and Debbie Joffe, who later became Ellis's wife, indicated that volunteers often did receive substantial help from these single brief sessions with Ellis. Most of them also found the suggestions offered by members of the audience helpful (Ellis & Joffe, 2002). Ellis further claimed that audience members were also helped by watching and listening to these single sessions, although this was never studied.

My interest in the Friday Night Workshops led me to serve as the therapist at some of these workshops, both while Ellis was alive and after his death,[5] during my many visits to the Albert Ellis Institute. From this experience, I discovered that I was very much drawn to working within a single-session format. From the informal feedback that I got from clients and audience members, my work was appreciated. Following on from this, I have given demonstrations in front of face-to-face and online audiences of what is effectively single-session therapy in that the client and I only have one session. I have done so in many different settings and countries.

Thus, whenever I give a workshop on a topic, I demonstrate how I work therapeutically with one or more volunteers who have a problem in the topic area under consideration or, if I am giving a more general workshop, volunteers are invited to come forward and discuss an issue of their choosing. The format is generally the same and derives from the Friday Night Workshop format, with an interview followed by observations and questions put to me as the therapist and to the client by audience members. In addition, I do two things. First, I digitally record the interview and offer a copy to the client.[6] Second, I have the recording transcribed and provide the transcription to the client on request. I keep a copy of both of these and consult them both as a means of self-supervision. I have incorporated both the digital voice recording (DVR) and the transcript into the Single-Session Integrated Cognitive Behaviour Therapy (SSI-CBT) approach that I have devised and which I will describe in this book.

I mentioned earlier that I was influenced by the Gloria–Kathy–Richard trilogy of films where leading therapists demonstrated CBT and non-CBT ways of working. I have subsequently made several DVD demonstrations of myself doing therapy with volunteer clients with problems such as procrastination and guilt, two areas in which I am interested. All these live and recorded demonstration single sessions have helped me over the years to refine my approach, culminating in the development of SSI-CBT.

So far I have discussed those influences on my ideas about SST that were predominantly demonstrative. In addition, my views have been shaped by what has happened in everyday practice. First, like many people in the SST field, I have been struck by the number of people over the years who have made an appointment at the end of the first session and have then cancelled it, saying that, on reflection, the first session was sufficient. While I have not canvassed these people from my caseload as comprehensively as Talmon (1990) did, those who gave reasons for not returning pointed to the first session helping them to do such things as: putting things into perspective, giving them a different way of thinking about the problem and its relevant factors, and seeing that they could deal with the issues involved better than they thought they could. As someone steeped in the cognitive-behavioural model, these reasons pointed to what could be done quickly if the conditions were right.

Second, I noticed over the years that some people use therapy very briefly but do so at various points over a long period. Thus, I have seen many clients come for one or two sessions and then stop, returning a long time later to discuss other issues and do so again very briefly. These people seem to benefit from a very brief intervention at different points of the life cycle. I have had to modify my practice to accommodate these people's therapeutic needs. I have been open to doing this rather than getting them to fit into an ongoing therapy Procrustean bed.

Finally, I encountered various situations with people that meant that I would only see them for one session if I took them on. Thus, several people have wanted to see me for one session because they did not want to commit themselves to further sessions. Also, some people in therapy wanted a second opinion on their situation, or their therapists recommended that I see them for such an opinion. Additionally, people who had heard about CBT wished to have a taste of it before committing themselves to a longer course of treatment (and not necessarily with me) and thus would only commit themselves to one 'taster' session. Because I have been happy to accommodate all of these requests, I have had to modify my practice accordingly.

In this introduction, I have provided a brief historical context of SST and discussed what has influenced my interest in this field, culminating in developing an approach that I have called Single-Session Integrated Cognitive Behaviour Therapy (SSI-CBT). Let me begin by describing its theoretical framework in the first part of this book before considering its practice in the second part.

Notes

1   In the UK, drop-in centres tend to be places where a person can come into a setting associated with the promotion of mental well-being, be greeted, invited to look around, peruse some reading material and if they want to talk to someone, that person may 'signpost' the person to

services that they may find helpful. Therapy tends not to take place in such 'drop-in' services. By contrast, in Australia, Canada and the USA, walk-in centres are places where a person can get therapy immediately for their stated concern.

2   Gloria did, however, correspond with Carl Rogers after her session with him (Burry, 2008).

3   These were initially billed under the heading 'Problems of Living' to convey the idea that help was being provided for everyday problems rather than for clinical problems.

4   And sometimes not so pertinent observations!

5   Since Ellis died, the tradition of carrying out single sessions of REBT in front of a public audience has continued under the new heading of 'Friday Night Live'. A number of trained and experienced REBT practitioners serve as the therapist at these events on a rotational basis. This has continued during the Covid-19 pandemic.

6   To get the digital voice recording (DVR) of the session, the person has to email me to request the copy, which I send via a Cloud service that provides the client with a download link. Such recordings are too large to send by email attachment.

Part I

THEORY

1

Single-Session Integrated CBT (SSI-CBT): What it is and some basic assumptions

When I developed a cognitive-behavioural approach to single-session therapy, I mainly crystallised my way of working that I had developed from the experiences I outlined in the Introduction. However, I also wanted to outline a framework that other CBT therapists could use who wanted to do single-session therapy in their way. In this book, I will discuss the general framework while illustrating the points with my particular approach. When I discuss the general framework, I will refer to it as SSI-CBT, and when I discuss my specific approach, I will refer to it as SSI-CBT (WD). My main goal is to focus on SSI-CBT, but many of the examples are taken from SSI-CBT (WD).

While CBT therapists who wish to use a single-session approach will no doubt develop their own format, at the moment my format is as follows:

- A person contacts me and requests explicitly single-session therapy, or a person contacts me and, after I have explained the services that I offer, they opt for SST
- Having agreed on a date to meet for the single session, I send the person a pre-session preparation form to complete and return before the session. This is designed to help the person get the most from the session. I used to do this by telephone, but no longer do so because it is not time efficient and adds to the cost of the process
- The session takes place, and
- A follow-up takes place at a time agreed between the client and me

DOI: 10.4324/9781003214557-3

While SST can be one session and one session only (see Introduction), more usually it is seen as:

> An intentional endeavour between the therapist and the client where the former helps the latter to take away what they have come for from the session, but where further help is available if needed.

As such, at any point it may become clear that the person may need more therapy, in which case you[1] may offer this. If you offer another single session or series of single sessions, this may be viewed as 'One-At-A-Time' Therapy (OAATT) (Hoyt, 2011), which some in the SST field see as synonymous with SST. However, when you and the client agree that they will have a block of therapy sessions or ongoing therapy, at that point the work is no longer considered single-session therapy.

What is SSI-CBT?

How can Single-Session Integrated Cognitive Behaviour Therapy (SSI-CBT) be summed up in a nutshell? I think the approach is characterised by the following:

- It is a perspective on SST that is broadly CBT in its foundations (from all waves). In my view, CBT is a tradition, not an approach, and SSI-CBT draws from a variety of CBT approaches
- SSI-CBT also draws upon relevant work from outside CBT. Thus, in my approach to single-session therapy that I refer to as SSI-CBT (WD), I am influenced by:
  - The work of leading single-session therapists, including Talmon (1990)
  - Solution-focused therapy (e.g. Ratner, George & Iveson, 2012)
  - Pluralistic therapy (Cooper & McLeod, 2011)

- Transformational chairwork (Kellogg, 2015) and
- Strengths-based approaches (e.g. Duncan, Miller & Sparks, 2004)
- It recognises the importance of behaviour and putting learning into practice
- It recognises the impact of various cognitions (e.g. inferences, attitudes/beliefs/schemas) expressed in several ways (words and images) at different levels of awareness
- It emphasises the importance of emotional impact
- It highlights the importance of the client taking away new meaning in a memorable form and which can be used in appropriate situations
- It is not a single approach to single-session work and is not protocol-driven. Instead, the therapist is encouraged to view each encounter as an unrepeatable event and respond to the client as a unique individual rather than a person with a diagnosable condition treated in a standard manner

An important note

I want to clarify that there are occasions when a person wants to use a single session of therapy *not* to solve a particular problem or deal with a specific issue. Instead, they may want to explore an issue or talk to get things off their chest. These are legitimate uses for a single session. Any SST practitioner (including an SSI-CBT therapist) needs to offer a helping stance to facilitate the client in these respects. However, they do not require the therapist to draw upon their skills as an SSI-CBT therapist, and, as such, they fall outside of the scope of this book. This does not mean that helping clients explore an issue or express their feelings is not valuable. Far from it. It is beneficial in that, by doing so, you are helping the client in the way that they want to be helped. Having made this point, this book focuses on situations where the client wants to solve a particular problem, get unstuck, make a decision, resolve a dilemma, or any other situation where there is a specific focus to the work. In such cases, I will discuss how you can use SSI-CBT to help clients with the issues for which they are seeking help.

The basic assumptions of SSI-CBT

Both the general SSI-CBT approach and my specific SSI-CBT (WD) approach are underpinned by several theoretical assumptions that I need to clarify so that you understand the foundation of this way of working.

This may be it

A vital assumption of all forms of SST is that the time you have with a client may be 'it', and therefore both parties need to appreciate this and work determinedly to get the most out of this time.

It's all here

If SSI-CBT were a play, then you and your client are the two protagonists, and the context plays a vital role in determining the focus of the action. These three ingredients are all that is necessary to help both parties get the most out of the process. Thus, 'it's all here'.

Focus on both the 'here and now' and the future

What makes CBT an approach that is a good fit with single-session therapy are its present-centred and future-oriented foci. While as an SSI-CBT therapist you might ask questions about a client's past, this would be to discover what the person has tried that was not effective – in which case you would encourage the client to distance themself from this, going forward – and what the person has done that has been helpful – in which case you might wish to encourage the client to capitalise on this, going forward. Generally, however, you will want to find out what the current issues are that the person wants help with and what the person will accept as a viable and realistic goal, given the single-session nature of the work.

Therapy starts before the first contact, and will continue long after the final contact

It is tempting to think that while SSI-CBT is very brief, all its therapeutic potential is realised through contact between therapist and client. This is not the case and, as an SSI-CBT therapist, it is important that you appreciate the therapeutic value of extra-therapy variables. Thus, just deciding that one wishes to address one's issues can be a powerful therapeutic force, as can contact with other people once such a decision is made.

> Leonard had experienced several losses and, for a while, had felt emotionally 'stuck'. He sought a single session from me, and, as is my custom, I sent him a pre-session questionnaire (see Table 19.1) to help him prepare for the session. The night before the session, Leonard had a Zoom conversation with some of his friends and told them how he felt after these losses. His friends all said that they had felt similar feelings after experiencing loss, which helped Leonard to 'normalise' some of his feelings and so, even before we had the session, Leonard began to feel far less stuck than hitherto.

Therapy occurs over the person's life cycle – it's not a one-shot deal

Throughout our lives, when we are physically ill, we will, in the first instance, consult our GP, who will manage our problem unless it appears more serious, in which case we will be referred for further investigation. However, this model of consulting a therapist as and when help is needed over the life cycle is regarded more suspiciously. However, SST therapists are generally comfortable with the idea of such consultations and will endeavour to help the person as quickly as possible within the SST framework.

Build on what's there, don't start from scratch

Clients generally come to SSI-CBT with a history of having tried various things to help them solve their problems. Therefore, rather than start from scratch, SST assumes that you can build on what clients have already tried to do to solve their problem, encouraging them to desist from using strategies that have not worked and to employ methods that have yielded some benefit and can be developed.

Clients are helped most by taking away one meaningful thing from the session rather than by being overloaded with too many takeaways

If you are working within a single-session framework, there is a temptation to want clients to go away with as much as possible so that they get the most out of the process. I call this the 'Jewish mother' syndrome, which points to the idea that the archetypical Jewish mother is only happy if their prodigal children leave after a visit during which they have eaten everything put in front of them, which is usually a considerable amount, and been given more food 'for later!' In the same way as a well-digested meal is more satisfying than leaving fully stuffed, single-session therapy clients who leave the process having digested one important therapeutic point, principle or method will generally get more out of the process than those armed with a plethora of such points, principles or methods, but without having digested any of them. Thus, aim to equip your SSI-CBT clients accordingly and resist the urge to throw everything, including the kitchen sink, at them.

Therapy is client-focused and client-driven

Like other approaches to SST, SSI-CBT is focused on the issue that the client brings to the session and what the client wants to take away from the session concerning this issue. You may have an idea of what the client is struggling with which is different from the client's view and if this happens, by all means share your view with the client. However, it is important that you do so in a way that the client feels able to accept or reject. While shared views are important in all therapy (see Chapter 3), the client ideally should feel happy that they are focusing on what they have decided is important, not on what you have decided is important.

The power is with the client

While SSI-CBT makes many demands on you to make skilful interventions in a short period, the real power to make this approach work lies with the client. To be effective as an SSI-CBT therapist, keep this point very much at the forefront of your mind. One of the best ways to implement this is to identify clients' strengths and encourage them to use these throughout the SST process and beyond. However, since you do have a significant contribution to make as a therapist, your real skill is to help your client make use of your contribution, using their strengths in doing so.

Expect change

In education, there is a principle known as the Pygmalion effect. This states that teachers who expect a lot from their students get more from them than teachers who expect much less (Rosenthal and Jacobson, 1968). Thus, go into SSI-CBT expecting change and convey this idea to your clients.

Complex problems do not always require complex solutions

If a client with complex problems wishes to engage in SSI-CBT, conventional clinical thinking would lead you to conclude that this mode of service delivery would not be suitable for them. However, as an SSI-CBT therapist, you will not think in this way. Instead, you don't know what the person wants to take away from the session, and you are open to the possibility that there may be a non-complex solution to a complex problem. You will also not forget that SSI-CBT includes the possibility that the client may wish to get further help for their complex problem later. With this safeguard in place, as an SSI-CBT therapist you will have nothing to lose by offering the person SSI-CBT, particularly if they are keen to access this service.

A journey begins with the first few steps

In my view, goals are central in SSI-CBT. I hold two major goals in mind when working with a client in SSI-CBT: the goal related to their nominated[2] problem (i.e. their problem-related goal) and what they want to take away from the session (i.e. their session goal). Quite often in SSI-CBT, when the client has achieved their session goal, they feel more equipped to pursue their problem-related goal independently. When this happens, they have taken the first steps towards a journey that they wish to make on their own. At other times they may want additional help to make this journey, which is perfectly possible in SSI-CBT since it signs up to the definition of SST that I presented at the beginning of this chapter.

Having defined SSI-CBT and discussed its major assumptions, in the next chapter I will outline what has been called single-session thinking (Hoyt, Young & Rycroft, 2020) or the single-session mindset (Young, 2018). Practitioners are advised to adopt this mindset to single-session work no matter what approach they take to it.

Notes

1   Throughout this book I will address you, the reader, directly as if you are already an SSI-CBT therapist. I felt most comfortable using this more personal 'voice' in this particular book and I hope that you don't mind.

2   In this book, I refer to the client's 'nominated' problem as the problem that the person wants to focus on during the session.

2

The single-session mindset in SSI-CBT

In my view, adopting what has been called the single-session mindset (Young, 2018) or single-session thinking (Hoyt et al., 2020, 2021) and applying this to the practice of SSI-CBT is one of the most critical tasks for you as an SSI-CBT practitioner. For if you bring what I call here 'conventional clinical thinking' to SSI-CBT, you will soon get tied up in knots and end up overloading the client.

Elements of the single-session mindset in SSI-CBT

In this section, I discuss those features that comprise the single-session mindset and contrast them, whenever possible, with their conventional clinical mindset counterparts.

Use time efficiently

One of the most important elements of the single-session mindset pertains to how you, as an SSI-CBT therapist, think about time concerning your work. This is shown in the following principles.

Provide help at the point of need

Help at the point of need involves the client being seen when they need to be seen. This contrasts with the usual practice of helping the client when an appointment becomes available for them to be seen – a feature of how conventional clinical thinking is operationalised.

DOI: 10.4324/9781003214557-4

Help at the point of need has the following features with which SSI-CBT practitioners agree:

- It is better to respond to client need by providing some help straight away rather than by waiting to provide the best possible help. Conventional clinical thinking leads to the client being assessed to receive the best and most appropriate help as determined by the assessor. In SST, given the primacy of client choice, the client can choose to access conventional therapy if they know and agree to the waiting time[1]

- Providing immediate help is more important than carrying out a full assessment or a case formulation. However, conventional clinical thinking suggests the importance of both of these activities before therapy begins

- Therapy can be initiated in the absence of a case history. My practice as an SSI-CBT therapist is to invite the client to tell me anything about their past that *they* think is essential for me to know in order to be able to help them in the session

- People have the resources to make use of help provided at the point of need

- As will be discussed later in this book in Chapter 8, the best way to see if a client will respond well to SSI-CBT is by offering it to them and, if they accept the offer, seeing how they respond. Thus, suitability is assessed experientially after the fact rather than before the fact, with precious time being devoted to therapy rather than, in this case, assessment of dubious value. This contrasts with the conventional clinical mindset, which argues in favour of assessing client suitability for services before assigning the 'best indicated' treatment for the client's diagnosed problem

- Therapy can be initiated immediately, and risk can be managed if this becomes an issue. One of the most common objections to the principle of 'providing help at the point of need' is the issue of risk management. In conventional clinical thinking, risk needs to be assessed before therapy proceeds. However, in SSI-CBT, risk is not assessed as a matter of course.[2] Instead, it is identified *if* it is an issue, and if so the session is devoted to ensuring the client's immediate safety

Ensure time is used well between appointment scheduled and session held

In my view, it is important for a client to be given an appointment as soon as possible after seeking SST. There will still be a time gap between the scheduling of the appointment and it being held. It is important that you use this intervening period well by suggesting that the client prepares to get the most from the session when they have it (see Chapter 19).

You do not have to rush

While time is at a premium in SST, the most effective single-session therapists seem to take their time and don't rush the process. However, it is vital that you work at the client's pace and help them stay focused on their nominated issue and the related goal/solution. If you rush the process, you will focus more on what you should cover than on helping the client.

Begin therapy from moment one

Walk-in single-session therapists have much to teach therapists who offer SSI-CBT by scheduled appointment. From the perspective of the efficient use of time, this means beginning therapy as soon as the client arrives and focusing the session on their stated wants. What has helped me see the importance of this in my regular SSI-CBT thera-peutic practice are the live single-session therapy demonstrations that I have done over my career (Dryden, 2018, 2019, 2021a, 2021b, 2021d). Here, I have a minimal period, approximately 25 minutes, to help someone with a problem for which they are seeking help. This work has helped me see the importance of cutting to the chase and cutting out talking about things that, while interesting, will not help the person with their stated wants. As a result, I now hold in mind the importance of beginning therapy from moment one with all my single sessions.

Transparency

It is vital that you keep in mind the need to be transparent about salient aspects of SSI-CBT. Thus, you will need to be transparent about the nature of SSI-CBT and what you can do and cannot do in the course of a single session. Because some people do not want any form of CBT, you need to clarify that CBT is the primary, but not the only, influence on your practice of SSI-CBT. It is vital that the person knows about the nature of SSI-CBT before they can be said to have given their informed consent to proceed.

How the SSI-CBT therapist approaches the session

Like other SST therapists, as an SSI-CBT therapist, you approach the session you will have with the client knowing that it could be the only session you will have. This is the case irrespective of any diagnosis the client may have or the complexity and severity of their problems. The experiences of those SST therapists working in walk-in clinics (see Slive & Bobele, 2011) have shown that people with severe and complex problems do come for single-session work and get as much from this work as those with less severe and complex issues.

From a conventional clinical perspective, a CBT therapist would approach the first session expecting it to be the first of a series of sessions. Therefore, the therapist would begin by taking a case history from the client, assessing what problems the person may have and negotiating with the client the order in which they should be tackled. If time permits, the therapist would begin developing a case formulation of the client's problems.

The major difference between the two mindsets here is that, when holding a single-session therapy mindset, the CBT therapist would begin therapy immediately (see above). However, when adhering to a conventional clinical mindset, they wouldn't.

There are CBT therapists who hold the view that it is vital to develop a case formulation before beginning to intervene with the client's problems. While this is a valid position to take when it is known that the client will commit themselves to a course of treatment, it is not good practice in SSI-CBT.[3] Furthermore, as noted elsewhere in this book, you never know, for sure, if a client will return for more sessions after the first session has been completed. Given this, as an SSI-CBT therapist, you approach the first session *as if* it could also be the last.

See the session as complete in itself

CBT therapists who wish to practise SSI-CBT do need to let go of the idea of protocol- or manual-driven treatment. While in longer-term therapy it may make sense to have a protocol of, for example, eight sequential sessions for the treatment of a particular problem, if the therapist tries to condense these sessions into one when the person has the same problem, then this is a recipe for disaster. Indeed, such an endeavour stems from what I am calling conventional clinical thinking. To best help this client in SSI-CBT, the therapist used to delivering manual-based CBT first needs to adopt a single-session mindset and see the single session as a whole, complete in itself. This means letting go of the idea of condensing a large number of sessions into one and instead taking from the protocol certain ideas that may help them to assist the client who is in front of them with their problem. As an SSI-CBT therapist, you do not look at the problem but at the person who has the problem. Doing so ensures you offer a bespoke form of help based on the client's stated wants rather than an off-the-peg protocol-based form of help designed for the problem irrespective of the person who has the problem.

Put the client at the centre of the process

Like other SST therapists, when bringing a single-session mindset to the work, you place the client at the centre of the therapeutic process as an SSI-CBT practitioner. This means that you hold in mind that the client decides which service to access since they are the best person to judge what they want from therapy. In this sense, SSI-CBT echoes the voices of therapy service users who argue that they want a greater say over their offered services. In addition, as an

SSI-CBT therapist, you are guided by the view that you need to ask the client what they want to achieve from the session and work with them to achieve this goal.

In addition, you recognise that, in effect, the client decides how many sessions to have and often opts to have one session. As Hoyt and colleagues (2020: 224) say, 'clients are far less interested in psychotherapy than are therapists and prefer brief therapeutic encounters'.

All this contrasts with the situation where the therapist operates according to a more conventional clinical mindset. Here, the therapist assesses the client and their problems and suggests a form of treatment based on that assessment, indicating how long that treatment should ideally last. While the client is consulted on such matters, the therapist takes the lead and makes suggestions. Here, the client is not at the centre of the process. I will discuss this vital principle further in Chapter 7.

No suitability assessment is needed

As I will show in greater depth in Chapter 8, single-session thinking suggests that as there is no reliable or valid way of determining who will benefit from SSI-CBT and who will not, spending time attempting to determine this at the outset is not a good use of therapeutic time. The only way to discover who will benefit from a CBT-influenced single therapy session is for you and your client to have a single therapy session and see if the client benefits from it. If they do not benefit from the session, as made clear in Chapter 1, further help is available. Since the single-session mindset stresses the importance of the client making decisions about what forms of help they wish to access (see the previous point), the main criterion for client suitability for SSI-CBT is that the client understands what the SSI-CBT practitioner is offering and wishes to access this form of help.

Focus on the client's internal strengths and values

In one session, it is unlikely that you will be able to teach the client skills that are not already in their repertoire. So instead it is important in SSI-CBT that you hold in mind the idea of helping them use what they do have in their repertoire. This involves you looking for opportunities in the session to ask the client to identify those strengths that they have that they can use to address their problem or issue. Examples of such strengths include perseverance, resilience, intelligence and empathy. Also, keep in mind that the client has values that potentially guide them, and at the right time it is important to ask them to articulate these values. Examples of such values include open-mindedness, honesty, loyalty and dependability.

You might be thinking about the difference between strengths and values. For me, *values* give direction to a person's goals, while the person draws on their *strengths* to help them to achieve these goals. As such, both a client's strengths and values are valuable resources in SSI-CBT.

Encourage the client to use external resources

In addition to drawing on the client's internal resources (strengths and values) in SSI-CBT, it is important that you keep in mind that there may be external resources that can help the person with their nominated problem/issue. An excellent example of such an external resource is people on the client's 'team' who may help them or support them to deal with their nominated issue. Here, different people may offer different types of help, as is the case with those involved with a professional tennis player (e.g. 'Team Nadal'). Other examples of external resources include organisations that offer help, phone 'apps' that may assist the client somehow, and, of course, a variety of search engines on the internet.

It is important to keep in mind the client's preferences for being helped

While the wish to focus on a pressing issue and look for a solution to this issue is perhaps the most common reason clients seek SSI-CBT, it is not the only reason. Sometimes a client may wish to explore an issue or seek to understand it with greater clarity or get things off their chest, and it is thus important for the SSI-CBT therapist to be flexible about which helping stance to adopt with a client. This means that the therapist may not need to use CBT insights in helping some clients in SSI-CBT! It is thus vital that the SSI-CBT therapist keeps this point in mind when doing the work.

Agree on a focus and keep to it

Whether a client wants help in finding a solution to a problem, in exploring an issue, in gaining a greater understanding of an issue or in making a decision (amongst others), it is crucial that you keep in mind the importance of helping the client to create a focus and then stick to it. The exception to this is when your client wants to talk uninterruptedly and wants you to listen to them. In which case, you need to show listening attention while the client talks about whatever they wish to discuss.

Keep in mind the 'PGS' principle

In SSI-CBT, we strive to do three things. First, we want to help the client nominate a problem for which they are seeking help. We also want to help them and ourself to understand this problem. I call this working with the 'P' in SSI-CBT, where 'P' stands for the 'problem'.

Second, we want to help the client to set a goal both in relation to the problem (problem-related goal) and for the end of the session (session goal). I call this working with the 'G' in SSI-CBT, where 'G' stands for the 'goal'.

Third, we want to help the person find and take away something to help them address their problem effectively and achieve their goal. If we can help the client rehearse this solution in the session and develop an action plan to implement it going forward, then so much the better. I call this working with the 'S' in SSI-CBT, where 'S' stands for the 'solution'. I keep the 'PGS' principle firmly in mind when I do SSI-CBT as it helps me structure the sessions that I do.

Help the client to take away what they can use – don't overload them

As an SSI-CBT therapist, you will keep in mind the importance of the client taking away from the session something of value that they can use going forward. In doing so, you will be guided by two related ideas: 'less is more' and 'more is less'. By contrast, when a therapist, usually new to SSI-CBT, brings a conventional clinical mindset to the single session, they will think, 'As I may not see the client again, let me give them everything they may need to deal with the problem going forward.' This therapist is guided by the idea 'more is more'. In acting on this idea, the therapist runs the risk of overloading their client, with the latter taking nothing away from the session. How much better for that client to have been helped to take away 'one thing' (Keller & Papasan, 2012) from the session that they could implement, and which could make a difference to their life. Effective SSI-CBT therapists keep in mind the importance of ensuring that their clients take away what is important to them (the clients) rather than to them (the therapists).

In this chapter, I discussed the single-session mindset that practitioners of SSI-CBT are encouraged to bring to the work and made some comparisons with what I called the 'conventional clinical mindset'. In the next chapter I will discuss working alliance theory, which I consider a practical generic framework for SSI-CBT.

Notes

1   In CBT, there are many empirically supported treatments for specific conditions lasting for a number of weeks and if the client wishes to wait for such a treatment rather than engage with SSI-CBT, their wish should be respected.
2   In some agencies where SST is offered, therapists are mandated to do a risk assessment with every client. In such cases, the therapist begins the session by explaining to the client that they have to do a risk assessment.

Here, they deal with any risk expressed or, if none is expressed, they focus on the client's stated wants from the session.

3   Jenkins (2020: 21) has outlined a one session case formulation CBT-oriented approach to SST based on 'reframing the nature of the client's difficulties and experience in terms of *possible* change and orienting the client towards *available* resources'. In my view, this approach is cautious in its aims and underestimates what can be achieved from a single session of therapy.

3

Working alliance theory: A generic framework for SSI-CBT

As is made clear in the title, Single-Session Integrated Cognitive Behaviour Therapy (SSI-CBT) is mainly based on cognitive behaviour therapy (CBT), a specific tradition within psychotherapy. However, as SSI-CBT is a flexible, open approach, it draws on concepts, ideas, practices and theories found in other therapy traditions and more generic therapeutic frameworks. One such framework that is particularly influential on how SSI-CBT therapists think about their work and how they practice is known as working alliance theory.

Working alliance theory was developed by Ed Bordin (1979), who argued that the practice of psychotherapy could be understood from the perspective of three broad interlocking domains: 'bonds', 'goals' and 'tasks'. Later, I added a fourth domain that I called 'views' (Dryden, 2011). In this chapter, I will present and discuss the updated version of working alliance theory and show how it influences the thinking and practice of SSI-CBT therapists.

Bonds

Bonds refer to the interpersonal connectedness between you and your client. There are several aspects of the bond domain that are relevant to SSI-CBT.

DOI: 10.4324/9781003214557-5

The 'core conditions'

The 'core conditions' is a colloquial term that stems back to Carl Rogers' (1957) view that there are a number of therapeutic conditions that need to be present for the client to grow psychologically and that these conditions are also sufficient for such growth to occur. There has been much debate concerning whether these conditions are necessary and sufficient, necessary but not sufficient, or even neither necessary nor sufficient (Ellis, 1959). Despite this, the prevailing view is that these conditions are core to the process of most approaches in counselling and psychotherapy, hence the term 'core conditions'.

When these core conditions are present, your client experiences you as empathic, respectful and genuine in their encounter with you. SSI-CBT considers that it is important for you to be experienced in these ways by your client. However, such experience is usually insufficient for change to occur unless it facilitates a relevant change in the client's meaning system and behavioural system that is considered a primary goal of SSI-CBT.

Therapeutic style

The core style of SSI-CBT is active and directive. Here, you actively direct your client's attention to the nature of their nominated problem and problem-related goal and the ways of thinking and behaviour regarded as playing a significant role in maintaining this problem. Then you work actively to help the client develop a change, preferably both in meaning and behaviour, to facilitate goal achievement. While it is vital for you as a therapist to adopt an active-directive style from the outset, it is equally important to strive to help your client be as active in the process as possible so that an outsider looking in would see a dialogue between two equally participating persons. When you are active and the client is passive, or vice versa, the chance of productive work taking place is diminished.

The therapist as authentic chameleon

Arnold Lazarus (1993) put forward the concept of the therapist as an 'authentic chameleon'. By this, he meant that effective therapists are prepared to change their therapeutic style with different clients but do so authentically. Thus, for example, it is possible to practise SSI-CBT with an informal or formal style, with humour or without, and to use stories, metaphors, parables, or not to do so. Unfortunately, there are no clear markers that can tell you which is the best style to use with a particular client, although, here as elsewhere, the modification of George Kelly's (1955) first principle is helpful to implement: 'If you do not know something about the client, ask them; they may tell you.'[1] Then, if you implement the answer and gauge the client's response, this will usually tell you whether you are on the right track.

Views

The views domain concerns the understandings that both you and your client have about the myriad issues concerning SSI-CBT. Leaving aside matters such as fees and confidentiality, the important issues that you both need to agree on if SSI-CBT is to be effective concern the following.

The components of SSI-CBT

It is vital that you both understand what the components are concerning SSI-CBT so that your client has accurate expectations of the process.[2] As I conceptualise it, SSI-CBT has the following components.

The initial point of contact

Here, the person contacts you, and you detail what SSI-CBT involves. If they wish to access SSI-CBT, the next point of contact is arranged.

The pre-session questionnaire

Here, you give the person a rationale for the completion of a pre-session questionnaire which will help them prepare for the session and which should be emailed back to you so that you can prepare for the session as well (see Table 19.1). The primary purpose of this part of the process is to help the client get the most from the session.

The session (face-to-face or online)

Before the Covid-19 pandemic, I did all of my SSI-CBT work face-to-face. The pandemic meant that this was impossible, and I did all this work by an online platform (e.g. Zoom). This enabled me to offer SSI-CBT to a much larger group of people and, in particular, those from different parts of the country and from abroad. From now on, I intend to offer clients a choice: to have the session face-to-face or online. Whichever medium is used, I tell the client that the session lasts *up to* 50 minutes and is where, in most cases, the bulk of the work is done. I draw your attention to the phrase 'up to' here since it is not uncommon for the client and me to complete our work before the end of a 50-minute session. Since it is crucial to end the session well (see Chapter 28), it is best to finish early if the work has been done than continue until the 50-minute watershed has been reached by filling in time. If you do the latter, you may detract from what the client takes away from the session.

The follow-up session

This session occurs at a date in the future selected by the client. It can be done over the telephone (in which case it lasts about 20 minutes) or by questionnaire (see Table 30.1).

While these four points of contact form part of the way I practise SSI-CBT, other therapists may use SSI-CBT differently. The critical point from the perspective of the views domain of the working alliance is that your client is clear about what they are getting and have given their consent to this.

The availability of additional sessions

Most theorists in the SST field argue that it is important to offer single-session clients additional sessions if they need them later (e.g. Talmon, 1990). In doing so, the argument goes, this relieves the tension that everything has to be achieved within one single session, which paradoxically enables the work to be done within this paradigm. The minority view is that it is important to be clear at the outset that in SST only one session is being offered so that the client knows exactly where they stand. From a working alliance perspective, what is important is that both you and your client are clear about whether additional sessions are possible and that you both proceed based on your agreed understanding of this view.

The cognitive-behavioural conceptualisation

SSI-CBT, by definition, employs a cognitive-behavioural conceptualisation of the client's problems and goals, although concepts from other frameworks may be additionally used. From a working alliance perspective, the work best proceeds when your client indicates that the CBT view of their problem makes sense to them and that they can make use of it. If not, SSI-CBT is unlikely to be effective. This does not mean that you cannot help the person. Rather, it means that you need to agree to the conceptualisation of the client's problem that makes sense to them and go forward based on this shared view.

Goals

SSI-CBT is both problem-focused and goal-oriented. When goals are considered from a working alliance perspective, what is important is that both you and your client agree on the client's goals. While this appears straightforward, it can be problematic when your client sets unrealistic goals given what can be realistically achieved from SSI-CBT. When this occurs, the extent to which you can help the client scale back their goals will determine the success of SSI-CBT.

I will discuss the complexity of goals in SSI-CBT and how to work productively with them in Chapters 9 and 23.

Tasks

Tasks are activities that both you and your client carry out in the service of the client's goals. From a working alliance perspective, important questions include the following:

- Can your client understand your interventions and the active-directive stance that you are taking?
- Can your client engage actively in the SSI-CBT process?
- Is your client prepared to engage with in-session tasks that may form a bridge between the discussion in the session and activity outside the session and may have an emotional impact on the client?

Affirmative answers to these questions indicate a strong alliance in the task domain and suggest a good outcome.

Developing and maintaining a good working alliance between you and your client is paramount in SSI-CBT. If the only way you can preserve that alliance is by straying outside the usual parameters of CBT, then I suggest that you do so.

While there is not a great deal of research on the working alliance in SST, there is an indication that those who benefit from a single session of therapy have a stronger working alliance with their therapist than those who do not benefit from such a session (Simon, Imel, Ludman & Steinfeld, 2012).

In this chapter, I have discussed the concept of the working alliance as a general way of thinking about the practice of SSI-CBT and what might be signs that SSI-CBT is being practised well. In the next chapter, I will consider the assumption of SSI-CBT that people primarily create and maintain their problems by a range of factors that are cognitive-behavioural in nature.

Notes

1   Kelly's (1955: 322–323) first principle was: 'If you do not know what is wrong with a person, ask him; he may tell you.'

2   At some part of the process, the therapist needs to be clear about confidentiality and its limits, the fee (if one is levied) and how it is to be paid, and any mandatory areas that the therapist has to cover. For example, in some agencies all therapists have to carry out a client risk assessment. The client gives their informed consent once they understand and agree to all these points and the points of contact discussed in the main body of the text.

4

People largely create and maintain their problems by a range of cognitive-behavioural factors

I mentioned in Chapter 1 that Single-Session Integrated Cognitive Behaviour Therapy (SSI-CBT) is best seen as an overarching framework that can accommodate different approaches within the CBT tradition. While these therapies differ in ways that I will discuss a little later, they all ascribe to the idea that people primarily create and maintain their psychological problems by employing a range of cognitive and behavioural factors.

The 'waves' of CBT

Hayes (2004) argued that the development of CBT could be seen in terms of a number of 'waves'. In using the SSI-CBT framework, first wave therapists, often seen as espousing a non-cognitively oriented behaviour therapy, will emphasise factors that explain the development and maintenance of psychological problems through classical conditioning, associative learning and positive reinforcement of disturbed responses.

'Second wave' CBT therapists will use the SSI-CBT framework by focusing much more on a range of cognitive factors at different levels within the cognitive system (such as negative automatic thoughts, thinking errors, dysfunctional assumptions and schemas). This echoes the idea that goes back to Epictetus that people disturb themselves not by things but by the view they take of things. Behaviour here is seen mainly as what the person does based on holding these 'views'. These therapists will seek to effect change

DOI: 10.4324/9781003214557-6

in the content of these cognitive factors, with changes in behaviour reinforcing this cognitive change.

'Third wave' CBT therapists will use the SSI-CBT framework to consider factors that reflect people's failed attempts to deal with 'normal' cognitive and emotive responses to adversities deemed problematic by the individual, resulting in the person adopting an overly critical stance towards self for these responses. 'Third wave' CBT therapists do not advocate that clients change their so-called 'dysfunctional' cognitive and emotional responses. Instead, they provide a rationale for them to adopt a mindful and compassionate acceptance of these responses, with value-based, goal-oriented behaviour being encouraged in the face of such acceptance.

In reality, therapists probably draw on all three 'waves' in developing their integrated practice of CBT.

SSI-CBT (WD)

I have mentioned that my primary task in writing this book is to show how CBT therapists practising various CBT approaches can use the SSI-CBT framework. I also said that I would illustrate the points that I make by outlining how I practise SSI-CBT. I refer to my approach as SSI-CBT (WD). So, in this section, I will outline the factors that I keep in mind when working with clients.

Rigid and extreme attitudes vs flexible and non-extreme attitudes

My foremost allegiance in CBT is to Rational Emotive Behaviour Therapy (REBT). The central theoretical tenet of this approach is that people disturb themselves about adversity by the rigid and extreme attitudes that they hold towards adversity. If they are to respond healthily to such adverse events, they need to be helped to develop flexible and non-extreme attitudes instead (Dryden, 2021e). Thus, within an SSI-CBT framework, I look for an opportunity to focus on the rigid and extreme attitudes that underpin my client's problems to help them make these attitudes flexible and non-extreme. If such attitude change is not possible, I will look for ways of assisting the client in other cognitive-behavioural ways, thus facilitating inference change, behavioural change or environmental change in problem-related situations.

> Jessica sought single-session therapy for her problems with social anxiety. She was anxious because she believed that she had to be interesting and that people would reject her if she wasn't, which she regarded as terrible. My choice points were to help Jessica develop a flexible attitude about the possibility of not being interesting and a non-extreme attitude about being rejected, or question her inferences (1) that she would/would not be interesting and (2) that people would reject her if she weren't interesting.

Avoiding vs confronting issues

People often unwittingly maintain their problems by their attempts to avoid them or avoid the distress that their problems occasion. This generally serves to keep them safe in the short term but does not help them long term. So, in dealing with clients' issues within SSI-CBT, I generally look for the following:

- Ways in which clients avoid troublesome situations
- What clients do to keep themselves safe if they cannot escape such situations, but without dealing with these situations constructively
- What clients tend to do to try to eliminate their troublesome thoughts and emotions
- What clients do to overcompensate for their problems
- Clients' attempts to deal positively or neutrally with adversity

Unhealthy vs healthy stances towards problems

When people develop problems, their stance towards these problems enables them to tackle them productively or gives them an additional problem about their original problem. When the latter occurs, these further problems are known as 'meta-problems'. It sometimes happens in SSI-CBT that when the client is helped to tackle their meta-problem, this is sufficient to allow them to live productively, even when what they see the original problem is still present.

Colin sought help for what he saw as his oversensitivity. He would become very emotional whenever he lost something or someone of value to him. Colin felt ashamed about his 'oversensitivity', which, it transpired, was his major problem. When I helped Colin to accept himself as an ordinary person who reacted more emotionally than he would have preferred and to acknowledge that he was not a weak person, he could stop ruminating about his 'over-responsiveness'.

Behaviour towards others

Quite often, people seek single-session therapy for help with interpersonal problems. How I deal with such situations is first to establish whether or not the person is disturbing themselves about the other person and, if so, to deal with this first. Then I discover how they have behaved towards the other person and how the other person has been treating my client. My focus here is to ascertain if my client is unwittingly perpetuating the problem by the way they are behaving towards the other person and, if so, to try to help the client bring about change by encouraging them to modify their behaviour rather than try to change the other person directly.

Discomfort unbearability vs discomfort bearability

In my experience, the ability to bear what might be broadly termed discomfort is important if a sustained therapeutic change is going to occur. Given this, I look for points where clients may hold discomfort unbearability attitudes and encourage them to hold and act on an alternative set of discomfort bearability attitudes (Dryden, 2022a). A particular type of discomfort unbearability refers to people's perceived ability to withstand their disturbed feelings and is known in the literature as 'distress intolerance' (Zvolensky, Bernstein & Vujanovic, 2011). Such intolerance leads people to try to tranquillise their distressing emotions and avoid situations in which they experience such feelings, thus significantly perpetuating the psychological problems. Helping clients to bear their distress is, therefore, an important goal in SSI-CBT.

In this chapter, I made the general point that SSI-CBT therapists draw from the different 'waves' of CBT to help them and their clients understand how the latter have been unwittingly maintaining their problems. I then outlined my approach to this issue in the way I practise SSI-CBT, which I refer to as SSI-CBT (WD) in this book. In the next chapter, I will discuss the principle of helping clients to face their adversities in SSI-CBT.

5

As far as possible, clients should be helped to deal healthily with the adversity involved in their problem, whether real or inferred

What adversities do clients discuss in SSI-CBT?

In my experience, SSI-CBT clients discuss similar adversities to those discussed by clients in ongoing therapy. Beck (1976), in an early work entitled *Cognitive Therapy and the Emotional Disorders*, outlined the kinds of adversities that tend to be associated with each of the main emotional problems for which clients seek help. In doing so, he introduced a concept he called the personal domain. This comprises people, objects, concepts and ideas that are important to a person. It also includes what is important to the person about themself. In 2009, I published an update of this model (Dryden, 2009), which I recently developed (Dryden, 2022b). In this update, I distinguished between two significant realms of the personal domain: the ego realm (which concerns the person's estimation of themself) and the non-ego realm (which involves everything the person holds dear which does not impinge on their self-estimation).

The cognitive-behavioural model of the emotions states that when clients present their emotional problems in SSI-CBT (at 'C' in the 'ABC' model),[1] they suggest what they are disturbed about at 'A' (i.e. what adversities they face or think that they face). Here is a list of the most common emotions that clients discuss in SSI-CBT and the associated adversities.

DOI: 10.4324/9781003214557-7

Anxiety

When a client presents with anxiety, they tend to be anxious about something that poses a *threat* to a central aspect of their personal domain. The important element of this threat is that it is perceived to be imminent. Common anxiety-related adversities in the ego realm of the personal domain include:

- Failure
- Rejection
- Criticism
- Disapproval; negative judgement from others
- Disclosure of negative information about self
- Lack of self-control

Common anxiety-related adversities in the non-ego realm of the personal domain include:

- Uncertainty concerning one's physical or mental well-being
- Doubt about the existence of purity related to a core aspect of the personal domain
- Lack of self-control
- Feeling uncomfortable

Depression

When a client presents with feelings of depression, they tend to be depressed about:

- Failure within their personal domain
- A loss from their personal domain
- Undeserved plight experienced by self or others

The core difference between anxiety and depression here is that in anxiety the adversity is imminent, while in depression it is deemed to have happened.

Guilt

When a client presents with feelings of guilt, they tend to feel guilty about:

- Breaking one of their codes within the moral sphere of their personal domain
- Failing to live up to one of their codes within the moral sphere of their personal domain
- Harming or hurting the feelings of others

Shame

When a client presents with feelings of shame, they tend to feel ashamed about:

- Falling very short of one of their ideals within their personal domain
- Revealing something 'shameful' about themselves
- Being judged negatively for a personal weakness within their personal domain
- Something 'shameful' being revealed by or about someone with whom one feels closely associated

Hurt

When a client presents with hurt feelings, they tend to feel hurt about:

- Being more invested in a relationship than the other person with whom they are involved
- Being poorly treated and undeservedly by another person with whom they are involved

Anger

When a client presents with feelings of anger, they tend to feel angry about several adversities which include:

- Being frustrated (e.g. being obstructed in the pursuit of a valued goal)
- Someone breaking one of their personal rules
- Them breaking one of their own personal rules (in self-anger)
- Another posing a threat to their self-esteem
- Another disrespecting them
- Being treated unjustly or seeing another person being treated unjustly

Jealousy

When a client presents with feelings of jealousy, they tend to feel jealous:

- When they think that a significant relationship that they have (usually, but not exclusively, romantic in nature) is being threatened by someone else's interest in the person with whom they are involved or by that person's interest in someone else
- When they face uncertainty or ambiguity concerning the above threat

Envy

When a client presents with envy, they tend to feel envious:

- When someone has something (e.g. an object, a relationship or a job) they want but don't have

When should you help clients deal with adversities in SSI-CBT?

The salient question here is: under what conditions should you, as an SSI-CBT therapist, help the client deal head-on with adversities rather than help them work around these adversities?[2] The answer to this question is complex, but in SSI-CBT (WD) I help a client deal directly with an adversity when:

The client is 'stuck' in the face of the adversity in question

Being 'stuck' here means that the client repeatedly responds to the same type of adversity in the same manner and cannot move on. When this happens, the goal of the intervention is to promote movement in the client, and this is best done, in my view, by helping them face up to and deal directly with the adversity, if at all possible.

The client reacts to the adversity with disturbed feelings or unconstructive behaviour

As practitioners of Acceptance and Commitment Therapy (ACT) note, the presence of negative feelings is not necessarily a sign that a client needs help to deal with an adversity (e.g. Batten, 2011). However, if they respond with disturbed negative feelings and particularly if this emotional response is accompanied by unconstructive behaviour, then the client will generally need to be helped to deal more constructively with the adversity. However, this certainly does not preclude them from experiencing negative emotions. One of the principles of REBT that underpins my approach to SSI-CBT (WD) is that healthy negative responses (feelings and behaviour) to adversity are based on the person holding flexible and non-extreme attitudes towards the adversity. In contrast, unhealthy negative responses to the same adversity are based on the person holding rigid and extreme attitudes towards the same adversity. Thus, I will only intervene if the person's response to adversity is negative and <u>un</u>healthy.

The client's main adversity is their response to their response to adversity

Humans are the only organism capable of disturbing themselves about their reactions to adversity. Sometimes this is their biggest problem, particularly when they respond negatively but healthily to the adversity in the first place.

> Marion lost her pet dog and felt sad about her loss. She cried a lot, and while she accepted that sadness was a normal response to this loss, she felt ashamed that her feelings of sadness remained with her for longer than she believed they should have done.

In addition, a client may feel disturbed about a disturbed reaction. This secondary disturbance needs to be nominated for change if its presence prevents you from dealing with the client's primary disturbance in SSI-CBT.

The client keeps responding unhealthily to adversity even when they correct their distorted inferences

Within a single-session therapy framework, it is always tempting to help people quickly by encouraging them to question their inferences about the situations they find troublesome, particularly when they are clear that these inferences are distorted.

> Dennis sought SSI-CBT for help with public-speaking anxiety. It quickly became apparent that he was anxious about being thought boring despite evidence to the contrary. The reality was that he got excellent feedback on his public presentations. In a previous, ongoing therapy, Dennis's therapist nominated for change his distorted inference that he was boring. However, while this helped Dennis in the short term, he kept returning to the idea that he would give a boring presentation. I took a different tack in SSI-CBT and encouraged him to face his adversity directly and imagine that he gave a boring speech. I then helped him to identify, examine and change the anxious meaning he attached to this eventuality.

I am not recommending that SSI-CBT therapists never question their clients' inferences. Indeed, sometimes when a client considers a new inferential point of view for the first time, it can bring about transformational change based on that 'aha' moment deemed the Holy Grail in SST (Armstrong, 2015).

A good friend and colleague of mine, Richard Wessler, used to give the example of a woman whom he tried to help deal with her unhealthy anger about what she saw as her father's intrusiveness. She would fly into a rage whenever her father rang and asked her, 'Noo, what's doing?' After getting nowhere by encouraging her to assume that her inference of paternal intrusiveness was true and helping her deal with this adversity, Wessler encouraged her to consider other meanings of her father's behaviour. The client's 'aha' moment came when Wessler asked her to consider her father's behaviour as his idiosyncratic opening interpersonal gambit – the modern equivalent being 'Whassup?' – and not as evidence of his intrusiveness. While this new inference was sustained, the question remains moot concerning what would have happened in the future if the client had obtained incontrovertible proof that her father was intrusive. In this case, working around the adversity was the best tack that this therapist could have taken with this particular client at that moment in time.

However, my view is that, whenever possible and feasible, clients should be helped to deal healthily with adversities that they find troublesome. Otherwise, what they achieve from SSI-CBT may be temporary. However, as we have just seen, there are exceptions to this principle.

In this chapter, I argued that whenever possible you, as an SSI-CBT therapist, should help a client deal with the adversity that featured in the problem. In the next chapter, I will discuss SSI-CBT's assumption that people can help themselves quickly if the conditions are right.

Notes

1   There are various versions of the 'ABC' model in CBT. In the one that I use, 'A' stands for an Adversity, 'B' stands for the person's Basic attitude towards the adversity and 'C' stands for the emotional, behavioural and thinking Consequences of 'B'.

2   In this section, while I present my clinical thinking, all decisions concerning what a client should ideally focus on are negotiated jointly between my clients and myself.

6

Human beings have the capability to help themselves quickly under specific circumstances

Albert Ellis (e.g. 2001), the founder of Rational Emotive Behaviour Therapy (REBT), whom I consider to be one of the most important influences on my career as a therapist, was fond of telling case vignettes to make a clinical point. The following vignette comes to mind whenever I talk about SSI-CBT and, in particular, our capacity to help ourselves in a short period as human beings.

The woman I will call Vera sought help for her elevator phobia from Albert Ellis. Because she could not afford individual therapy sessions, she joined one of Ellis's groups. While Vera accepted the idea that she needed to confront her fear by going on elevators, she resisted acting on this idea. This was the case despite the efforts of Ellis and her fellow group members to identify and deal with all the obstacles that she erected to prevent herself from actually entering an elevator. Throughout this, Vera maintained that she really wanted to overcome her elevator phobia.

Vera booked an individual session with Ellis one day late on a Friday afternoon, which was a very unusual occurrence. She had just heard that the company she worked for was moving their office suite from the fifth floor of a skyscraper to the 105th floor of the same building. Moreover, they were moving over the weekend and planned to be up and running in their new suite early on Monday morning. Hitherto, Vera had been

DOI: 10.4324/9781003214557-8

able to climb the five flights of stairs, but there was no way, she reasoned, that she could climb 105 flights of stairs every day. Vera was desperate to keep her job and implored Ellis to help her deal with her fear so that she could take the elevator to the 105th floor on Monday morning. Ellis told her that if she wanted to achieve her goal, she would have to commit herself to going up and down elevators in tall skyscrapers all weekend while accepting the significant discomfort of doing so. Vera did just that until she got over her fear. Repeated practice proved effective, as it would have done years earlier when Vera first sought therapy, but she did not engage with it at that time.

Before Vera made a very rapid change after her company announced the change of their office suite, you might be forgiven for thinking that she was not capable of helping herself in a short space of time with her elevator problem. However, it transpired that Vera did have that capability but only decided to use it under a particular set of circumstances. These seemed to be as follows:

Knowledge

Vera knew what she needed to do to overcome her elevator phobia. She had the requisite *knowledge.* When a client knows what to do to help themselves with a problem, this is an important ingredient for change but, as we have seen with Vera, not a sufficient one. Vera knew what she needed to do before the office suite move but decided not to act on that knowledge.

A committed reason to change

Before the office suite move, Vera claimed that she wanted to tackle her elevator phobia, but her actions belied her words. My explanation for this is that she did not have sufficient reason to address her problem properly before the move, but afterwards she did. She considered that getting to work by elevator to the 105th floor was the only way of retaining her job, which she was very keen to do. She further considered that the only way she could do that was to overcome her elevator phobia. Before the move, she was prepared to walk up to the fifth floor. If Vera had decided to change job, she would probably have remained half-hearted in her approach to tackling her phobia.

Some might say that before she learned of the office move, Vera lacked sufficient motivation to change. While I can understand this, my view is that the concept of 'motivation' is a little imprecise for our purposes as it tends to encompass a reason to change and a state of feeling, as when someone says: 'I did not do it because I did not feel motivated to do it.' My view on Vera's case is that when she learned of the office move and that she could lose her job if she did not take the elevator, she had a reason to change, to which she was fully committed. I call this having a *committed reason to change*, and when humans have this, they can do things that they and others may not think they are capable of doing.

Prepared to accept the costs of change

When Ellis told Vera that if she wanted to make a rapid change, then she would need to tolerate quite a lot of discomfort while undertaking the repeated practice that this approach required, he was asking her to consider whether or not she was prepared to accept the costs of change. 'No gains, without pains', as Benjamin Disraeli said. Experiencing discomfort is one of many costs that clients may encounter when they change, and it is important to help them identify what these costs are and reflect on whether or not they are *prepared to accept the costs of change*. Clients who want to make a rapid change, but are not prepared to accept the costs of doing so, will not benefit much from SSI-CBT.

These three ingredients – knowledge, having a committed reason to change and being prepared to accept the costs of change – need to be present for people to get the most from Öst's intensive one-session treatment of single phobias (see Davis III et al., 2012). Indeed, if all three are not present or their presence cannot be encouraged, clients who lack them may not be accepted into this intensive treatment programme.

Humans are capable of what Miller and C'de Baca (2001) have called 'quantum change'. These are sudden insights and spiritual-type epiphanies that occur within a short time but have lasting positive effects. While such change rarely happens within an SSI-CBT context, it demonstrates our capability as humans to make profound changes quickly. This makes it a core theoretical idea behind SSI-CBT.

In this chapter, I noted that we can change quickly if the conditions are right for it to happen. In the following chapter, I will discuss the importance of privileging your client's viewpoint in SSI-CBT.

7

It is important to privilege your clients' viewpoints in SSI-CBT

I remember reading the following sentence in an abstract of a journal article which has stayed with me. The study looked at various predictors of dropout and outcome in cognitive therapy for depression in a private practice setting (Persons, Burns & Perloff, 1988: 557). The sentence read as follows: 'In spite of significant improvement, 50% of patients terminated treatment prematurely.' While this statement can be read in a number of ways, it shows that a significant number of clients in this study left therapy once they had made significant improvement, while the authors considered that these clients had ended therapy prematurely. Of course, therapists have their views concerning client functioning and dysfunctioning and these views are coloured by professional knowledge. Maluccio (1979), in his classic study, found that therapists were less happy than their clients were when the latter terminated 'prematurely' because, while the latter were happy with what they had achieved, the former could see all manner of issues that needed to be dealt with but weren't. However, the point here is that, in single-session work, it is vital to prioritise your client's view over your own as a therapist. While you may see areas that your clients need to work on, it is important that you let them be the principal judge of what it is in their interests to address.

DOI: 10.4324/9781003214557-9

'Dropout'

In a comprehensive review of client variables in therapy, Bohart and Wade (2013) note that what complicates the literature on so-called therapy 'dropout' is that we have no agreed definition of premature termination or what they term 'early termination' (ET). I have already mentioned one somewhat tongue-in-cheek definition: 'dropout occurs when the client leaves therapy before the therapist thinks they are ready to'. More seriously, Bohart and Wade's review shows that while quite a few clients most certainly do leave therapy before they have benefited from the process, a good number also seem to end therapy because they have got what they wanted from the process. Thus, Westmacott, Hunsley, Best, Rumstein-McKean and Schindlera (2010) found that clients who terminated therapy without agreement with their therapists saw their psychological distress as less severe when they left therapy than when they entered into it, while their therapists rated their distress as unchanged. This echoes Maluccio's (1979) finding that clients were happier with what they got from therapy than their therapists were and thus left when they were ready to, but before their therapist believed that they should.

Therapists distinguish between clinically significant and non-clinically significant improvement, but clients tend not to make such a distinction for themselves. Barrett, Chua, Crits-Christoph, Connolly Gibbons and Thompson (2008), in their review, concluded that some clients end therapy satisfied even when they have not met their therapists' criterion of having made clinically significant change. Cahill, Barkham, Hardy, Rees, Shapiro, Stiles and Macaskill (2003) found that most clients in their study who left therapy without mutual agreement with their therapists achieved reliable non-clinically significant improvement, but few made clinically significant changes. This again suggests that these clients were far less concerned with making the latter type of change than were their therapists. In their review of research related to single-session therapy (discussed below), Hoyt and Talmon (2014b: 495) concluded that 'studies have reported a significant reduction of distress and problem severity, as well as improvements in client satisfaction, after a single session'. This suggests that clients are satisfied with what therapists would regard as non-clinically significant improvement, but which from the clients' perspective may be experienced as clinically significant.

While clients may be satisfied with what therapists define as non-clinical improvement, they can even achieve clinically significant improvement quickly. Thus, Barkham, Connell, Stiles, Miles, Margison, Evans and Mellor-Clark (2006) found that half of their client sample achieved a reliable and clinically significant change in their symptoms after one or two therapy sessions.

Hoyt and Talmon

Michael Hoyt and Moshe Talmon have long been at the vanguard of making a case for the clinical utility of single-session therapy. In a research-based overview relevant to SST, Hoyt and Talmon (2014b) asserted the following:

1. 'The most common (modal) length of therapy is one visit with 20%–58% of general psychiatric/psychotherapy patients not returning for better or worse after their initial visit' (p. 493).[1] Thus, whether therapists like it or not and for better or for worse, clients most frequently only attend one therapy session. This suggests that we should prepare for this eventuality in the way we approach work with new clients

2. 'From clients' point of view, a single session is often what is needed' (p. 493)
   - Between 27 and 42% of clients chose to attend for a single session even though they could have had more (Carey, Tai & Stiles, 2013; Weir, Wills, Young & Perlesz, 2008)
   - In several studies of SST, for approximately 60%, a single session is judged sufficient by the clients

As it is a guiding principle that we should privilege the client viewpoint in SST, we need to listen to what they are saying to us with their behaviour

3. Concerning treatment length, 'clients usually expect a shorter course than do their therapists' (p. 494). Whenever prospective clients approach me, they are keen to know how many sessions they need to attend. They often want to attend for very brief therapy rather than ongoing work

4. 'Patients have benefited by being allowed to simply walk-in or "drop-in" for a single session without a scheduled appointment when they wanted to meet with the therapist' (p. 495)

5. 'The efficacy of SSTs is not restricted only to "easy" cases but can have more far reaching effects in many areas, including treatment of alcohol and substance abuse as well as self-harming behaviour' (p. 503)

Many therapists object that SST is only for so-called 'easy' cases when learning about single-session therapy of whatever type. As Hoyt and Talmon (2014b) show in their review, this is not borne out by the data.

The data I have presented here appear to be in accord with a fundamental theoretical principle of SSI-CBT: namely that when the client viewpoint is privileged, clients often indicate to us that they want to be helped as quickly as possible. This book is based on the idea that there is much to be gained by giving them what they want.

In the following chapter, I will consider what is known as the suitability question for SSI-CBT.

Note

1   All page numbers in this section refer to Hoyt and Talmon (2014b).

8

Dealing with the suitability issue

One of the most frequently asked questions by professionals about SSI-CBT concerns the indications and contra-indications for this approach. In the first edition of this book, I engaged with this question (Dryden, 2017).

My previous position on the suitability issue (Dryden, 2017)

Who is suitable for SSI-CBT?

This is what I had to say about the suitability issue in the first edition of this book. I argued that the following were positive indications that a person would benefit from SSI-CBT.

People seeking help for non-clinical problems

1. People experiencing common, non-clinical emotional problems of living (problematic forms of anxiety, non-clinical depression, guilt, shame, anger, hurt, jealousy and envy)
2. People seeking help for relationship issues at home and work
3. People experiencing everyday problems of self-discipline
4. People ready to take care of business now and whose problem is 'non-clinical' but amenable to a single-session approach
5. People who are stuck and need some help to get unstuck and move on

DOI: 10.4324/9781003214557-10

6. People with 'clinical' problems but who are ready to tackle a 'non-clinical' problem
7. People with life dilemmas and quandaries
8. People who need to make an important imminent decision
9. People who are finding it difficult to adjust to life in some way
10. People with meta-emotional problems
11. People who view therapy as providing intermittent help across the life cycle
12. People who require prompt and focused crisis management

People seeking help for clinical problems

1. People with simple phobias willing to engage in intensive exposure (Davis III et al., 2012)
2. People with panic disorder willing to engage in immediate exposure after psychoeducation (Reinecke et al., 2013)

Coaching

1. People who are doing OK in the various aspects of their lives but have a sense that they could get more out of their lives
2. People who are looking to fulfil their potential

Prevention

1. People who have had a warning that they need to take action to prevent the development of a problem

Psychoeducation

1. People who are open to therapy, but want to try it first before committing themselves
2. People seeking advice on how CBT would tackle their problem

3. People who are reluctant about seeking therapy and are only prepared to commit to one session
4. Therapy trainees who want to find out what it is like to have therapy from a different perspective

Other contexts

1. Clients in therapy who are seeking a second opinion (or their therapists are)
2. Clients in ongoing therapy who want brief help with a problem with which their therapist can't or won't help them
3. People who volunteer for a demonstration session before an audience
4. People who volunteer for a videotaped demonstration session
5. People who are suitable for short-term CBT may also be suitable for SSI-CBT (see Safran, Segal, Vallis, Shaw & Samstag, 1993)

Who is unsuitable for SSI-CBT?

In addition, in the first edition of this book, I argued that the following were negative indications that a person would benefit from SSI-CBT.

1. People who find it challenging to connect with or trust a therapist quickly
2. People who request ongoing therapy
3. People who don't want CBT of any description
4. People who need continuing therapy
5. People who have vague complaints and can't be specific
6. People who are likely to feel abandoned by the therapist
7. People who are not suitable for short-term CBT are generally not suitable for SSI-CBT (see Safran et al., 1993). In the next chapter, I will discuss the assumption of SSI-CBT that a focus on both problems and goals is important

My current position on the suitability issue

Looking back at the time when I wrote the above for the first edition of this book (Dryden, 2017), it is clear that I was operating from what I call the 'conventional clinical mindset' where a lot of time is devoted to assessing a person in order to determine the best therapy approach for them. In doing so, I realise that I was developing a single assessment session to determine who was and who was not suitable for SSI-CBT. This is problematic for several reasons.

First, therapists are not good at determining who will attend for one session of therapy and who will attend for more and who will benefit from SST and who will not (Young, 2018). Instead, the only way to discover who will benefit from SST is to offer the person a single session and see if they will benefit. As this is the case, there is no point in the therapist setting suitability criteria that potentially serve as entry points into SST since attempting to do so prevents people from accessing single-session services.

Second, in general SST argues that it is best to begin therapy from the outset rather than devoting time to a suitability assessment with dubious validity and reliability. These two points are central features of what is known as the 'single-session' mindset (Young, 2018). The following is my favourite quote in the entire SST literature. While the quote is specifically about walk-in SST, its message applies to the SST field more generally, including SSI-CBT. It helped me to shift from conventional clinical thinking to single-session thinking on the suitability question.

> [Walk-in therapy]...enables clients to meet with a mental health professional at their moment of choosing. There is no red tape, no triage, no intake process, no wait list, and no wait. There is no formal assessment, no formal diagnostic process, just one hour of therapy focused on clients' stated wants... Also, with walk-in therapy there are no missed appointments or cancellations, thereby increasing efficiency.
>
> (Slive, McElheran & Lawson, 2008: 6)

I learned two things from this quote. First, I realised that the client decides to come for a single therapy session provided in a walk-in clinic. Professionals have no say in this matter. They cannot stop anyone from walking into the clinic. As such, no inclusion or exclusion criteria are employed. Second, I learned that therapy begins very soon after the person arrives at the clinic. These points persuaded me, and they freed me to focus on what matters in SSI-CBT: to structure the session to help the client get the most from the session rather than determine who is suitable for the session.

It may turn out that the client does not benefit from the single session, but the safeguard in SSI-CBT and other approaches to SST is that further therapy is available to the person if needed. This means that the person can access more suitable services due to having had a single session. As a consequence, I have come to believe two things:

1. The best form of assessment of who can and cannot benefit from SSI-CBT is for the person to have the single session
2. If the person needs further help, having a single session will help both client and therapist determine the best form of assistance for that person amongst the services provided by the agency or the private practitioner. The possibility of referral to available services provided by related agencies and other practitioners in independent practice should also be factored in here where relevant

While I am happy now to offer SSI-CBT to anyone who wants it, the person requesting it must fully understand this service's nature. Thus, here is what I say to people before we make an appointment:

'Single-session therapy is designed to help you and I focus on the issue for which you are seeking help and on helping you take away what you have come for from the session. If you

> need further help, it is available to you. My main influence in
> SST is cognitive behaviour therapy, but as I am flexible in my
> practice, I draw upon other therapeutic approaches too.'

I do not offer SSI-CBT to anybody who does not want SST or any form of CBT. Given this, SSI-CBT is an ethical approach because it is based on the client giving informed consent to proceed.

In this chapter, I presented my previous stance on the suitability of clients for SSI-CBT. I also gave my current position, explaining the shift from the former to the latter. In the next chapter, I will discuss the problem-, solution- and goal-focused nature of SSI-CBT.

9

A focus on problems, goals and solutions is important in SSI-CBT

As I briefly showed in Chapter 2, SSI-CBT is best seen as a problem-focused, solution-focused and goal-focused approach to single-session therapy. It differs from single-session therapy based on solution-focused lines, for example, which tends to steer clients away from their problems and orients them instead towards solutions or preferred futures.

Focus on problems

When considering problems in SSI-CBT, you should be mindful of the client-centred nature of the work. Consequently, if your client is seeking help for a specific problem, you should focus on this problem unless you have a good reason not to do so. I call this the client's 'nominated' problem. If the client wants help with more than one problem, you should encourage them to choose one. While this will usually be the problem that they are most concerned about, this may not be the case. When the client's nominated problem is assessed, if possible you need to understand both a specific example of this problem and its general nature. If you focus on too specific an example of the problem, then your client will not be helped to generalise learning from the example. Similarly, if you focus on the problem at too general a level, your client will not be assisted to engage emotionally in problem assessment and exploration.

DOI: 10.4324/9781003214557-11

My suggestion is that, if possible, it is best to identify the general nominated problem and a specific example of it. Here is an illustration of what I mean.

General nominated problem: I get walked over by people close to me.

Specific example: I got walked over by my aunt the last time I visited her.

'AC'-based problem focus

Once the client has nominated a problem and you have helped them to put it in its general and specific context, then you need to engage with the client in the process of understanding the nature of the problem (i.e. the client's emotional and behavioural response) and to which adversity the person is responding. In SSI-CBT, this means inviting your client to give their views on this issue as well as providing your own as a CBT therapist. As I mentioned in Chapter 5, most CBT therapists employ an 'ABC' framework when assessing their clients' problems. As different therapists use different versions of this 'ABC' framework, I will discuss a generic version for illustrative purposes. In this version, 'A' stands for an adversity, 'B' stands for the client's belief or thinking, and 'C' stands for the person's emotional and behavioural response to the adversity. Remember also from Chapter 5 that the person's emotional problem (at 'C') suggests what type of adversity they are facing or think they are facing. When you adopt a problem focus as an SSI-CBT therapist, you effectively utilise the 'A' and 'C' components of this framework. You will focus on the cognitive component of the 'ABC' framework a bit later in the process. Effective SSI-CBT therapists learn which adversities tend to go with which emotions and use this as a guide when focusing on the client's nominated problem (see Chapter 4). The following dialogue illustrates this:

> *Client:* I just get trod on because I'm just scared of upsetting my aunt if I stand up to her.
>
> *Therapist:* What's threatening to you about upsetting her?
>
> (*Here, the therapist is using their knowledge that when a person is scared, it is because they are inferring the presence of something threatening to their personal domain*).
>
> *Client:* Well, if I upset her, then I will torment myself.
>
> *Therapist:* With guilt?
>
> *Client:* Absolutely.
>
> (*Again, the therapist uses their knowledge concerning which emotion is suggested when a client finds upsetting somebody's feelings a problem and uses this knowledge to guide their intervention*).

It is a moot point concerning how formal you need to be in using the 'AC' components of the 'ABC' framework. This is partly a stylistic question for you, as a therapist, but it also concerns how valuable the client would find using this framework formally.

If the above therapist had utilised the 'AC' components of the 'ABC' framework format formally with the above client's nominated problem, it would have looked like this:

'A': Upsetting my aunt
'B': Not known yet[1]
'C' (Emotional): Guilt
(Behavioural): Not standing up for myself

Focus on goals

As briefly noted in Chapter 2, in SSI-CBT we distinguish between session goals and problem-related goals. Ideally, you should help the client see that achieving their session goal should ideally help them achieve their problem-related goal, although you will only be able to do this once you have helped your client set the latter goal.

Session goals

As the term clarifies, a session goal is a goal that the person nominates to achieve by the end of the session. You can ask for it after the person has selected a problem to discuss or at the very beginning of the session.

Here is an example of a session goal. The dialogue features a question that I recommend that SSI-CBT therapists use in enquiring about a goal.

Therapist:	Tonight, when you reflect on the conversation that we are going to have, what would you like to have achieved that would have made it worthwhile you coming to see me?
Client:	Learning some tools to help me deal with upsetting people like my aunt.

In response to questions about session goals in SSI-CBT, clients frequently say that they would like tools to deal with the problem, better understand the problem or look at things differently. I regard such statements as embryonic forms of a solution (to be discussed below).

Problem-related goals

Once you have helped the client set a session goal and the nature of the client's nominated problem has been understood, the next step is to help the client set goals concerning that problem. This is more complex than it appears at first sight. In particular, when asked about their goal, clients will usually respond with either an absence of a negative emotion or a positive way of behaving. They would usually not refer to the adversity that appears in their problem.

> *Therapist:* So you get trod on by people like your aunt because you would feel very guilty about hurting her feelings if you were to stand up to her. Is that right?
>
> *Client:* Pretty much.
>
> *Therapist:* What would you like to achieve in discussing this problem with me?
>
> *Client:* I would like to stand up for myself.
>
> (*Here, the client has nominated a positive behaviour for their goal. However, note that they have not specified a goal concerning how to deal with the situation where they upset their aunt. At the moment, they would feel guilty about doing so and, to avoid feeling guilt, they back down. So, the therapist has to do something tricky here: to work with the client's stated goal – to stand up for themself – and to help them set a goal concerning upsetting their aunt's (and others') feelings).*

Thus, it is important to help clients set goals in the face of adversity before assisting them in reaching their stated goals when these goals do not refer to the adversity in question. In the above example, the therapist proceeds thus:

Therapist:	OK, so you would like to stand up for yourself, and I will certainly help you do that. However, given that you feel guilty about the prospect of upsetting people like your aunt when you do stand up for yourself, do you think that it would be wise if I first helped you to deal better emotionally with upsetting her?
Client:	Yes, that makes sense.
Therapist:	So, I need to help you experience an emotion that is negative given that, for you, upsetting people is negative, but one that does not stop you from standing up for yourself.
Client:	Couldn't you help me to stand up for myself so that I don't upset people?

(*This is quite common. The client wants to find a way of achieving their goal without facing the relevant adversity. Sadly, this is not possible as no matter how skilfully they stand up for themself, the other person may be upset with them*).

Therapist:	Well, I will certainly try to help you to stand up for yourself in a way that minimises the chance that the other person will become upset with you, but do you think you can eradicate that as a possibility?
Client:	I guess not.
Therapist:	Would it make sense for me to help you deal with the possibility that the other person will become upset with you but do so without stopping you from standing up for yourself if that happens?
Client:	Yes.
Therapist:	As I said before, I need to help you experience an emotion that is negative given that, for you,

	upsetting people is negative, but one that does not stop you from standing up for yourself. Right?
Client:	Right.
Therapist:	Your feelings of guilt about upsetting people like your aunt stop you from standing up for yourself. What emotion about upsetting them would be negative in tone but would not stop you from asserting yourself?
Client:	Being sorry, but not guilty.
Therapist:	Excellent, so shall I help you do that in the first instance?
Client:	Yes, please, if you can.

'AC'-based problem-related goal focus

I mentioned above the 'AC' components of the 'ABC' framework drive the therapist's focus on the client's nominated problem. They also drive the therapist's focus on the client's goal concerning that nominated problem. The therapist ensures that the client sets a goal concerning the adversity at 'A' rather than bypassing the 'A'. In the above example, the therapist shows how to respond when the client tries to factor out the adversity in their goal-setting.

If the above therapist had utilised the 'AC' components of the 'ABC' framework format formally with the above client's goal, it would have looked like this:

'A': Upsetting my aunt
'B': Not known yet[2]
'C' (Emotional): Sorry rather than guilt
(Behavioural): Standing up for myself

Focus on solutions

Chapter 2 defined a solution as 'something that will help [the client] address their problem effectively and achieve their goal'. Several factors can contribute to this solution, and you need to keep the following in mind when helping the client to construct a solution in the session:

- The client's views on what constitutes a good solution
- Your views as an SSI-CBT therapist on what constitutes a good solution determined by your CBT-based assessment (see Chapters 10 and 11)
- Relevant client strengths and values (see Chapter 13)
- Appropriate external resources (see Chapter 13)
- What was helpful from the client's previous attempts to deal with the nominated problem
- What was helpful from the client's attempts to deal with other problems (both related to and unrelated to the nominated problem)

Put graphically, we have:

Problem ————————————→ Solution ————————————→ Goal

I will discuss the critical topic of helping clients to develop solutions in SSI-CBT in Chapter 25.

This chapter discussed the three foci therapists take in SSI-CBT: a problem focus, a goal focus, and a solution focus. In the next chapter, I will discuss the role of problem assessment and case formulation in SSI-CBT.

Notes

1   Note that the 'B' section is not yet known. This section is assessed once the nominated problem and the goal with respect to that nominated problem have been identified and agreed (see Chapters 10 and 11).

2   Note again that the 'B' section is not yet known. As before, this section is assessed once the client's nominated problem and the goal with respect to that nominated problem have been identified and agreed (see Chapters 10 and 11).

10

Carry out a full assessment of the client's nominated problem drawing on case formulation principles

In the previous chapter I discussed how, as an SSI-CBT therapist, you could use the 'AC' components of the 'ABC' framework introduced in Chapter 5 to identify your client's nominated problem and their goal concerning this problem. In this chapter, I will discuss the role of assessment and case formulation in SSI-CBT. In my view, you need to do a comprehensive assessment of the client's nominated problem drawing upon case formulation principles (meaning understanding the mechanisms which account for the client's issues from a broader perspective). However, you do not have the time to do a full case formulation in the time available to you, and, in my view, you do not need to do so.

It is important to understand assessment and case formulation in the context of other SSI-CBT tasks. Once you and your client have agreed that SSI-CBT is suitable for the latter, you need to do the following: (1) identify and agree on the client's nominated problem; (2) identify and agree on the client's goal with respect to this problem; (3) assess the problem and formulate the mechanisms that account for the continuing existence of the problem; (4) identify a central focus that can be nominated for change; (5) work to effect change in this central focus; and (6) encourage the client to rehearse change in the session in some meaningful way. Throughout this process, you need to ally the client's strengths with what you have to offer the client. Because time is at a premium in SSI-CBT, you need to decide what to include and what to leave out since you do not have the time to be all-inclusive in SSI-CBT. Your decisions

DOI: 10.4324/9781003214557-12

on this point will vary from client to client and will be informed by what the client wants to achieve from SSI-CBT.

Assessment of 'B' in the 'ABC' framework

You will recall from the previous chapter how you can use the 'A' and 'C' components of the 'ABC' framework to help you and your client identify and understand both the nature of the client's nominated problem and their goal concerning this problem. After this has been done, you are ready to assess the client's cognitions at 'B'.

Different CBT therapists will have different ideas about what cognitive activity to focus on when assessing 'B'. For example, those following the ideas of Aaron T. Beck will determine the presence of negative automatic thoughts (NATs), intermediate beliefs often expressed in the form 'if–then' and core schemas. Typically, in ongoing CBT of this type, the therapist moves slowly from the more surface level of NATs to the intermediate level and thence to the core schemas. However, such slow-paced assessment is not possible in SSI-CBT, so Beckian CBT therapists need to make a judgement call concerning what to focus on and what to omit when practising SSI-CBT.

Those therapists who practise Acceptance and Commitment Therapy (ACT) will focus on the thoughts with which their clients struggle. In this form of CBT, it is the struggle that clients have with their thinking rather than the thinking itself which is regarded as problematic. Thus, ACT therapists will tend to identify cognitions not with the view of changing them but with a view to assessing the struggle mechanisms that clients themselves employ in their attempts to change or eliminate these cognitions.

My approach to single-session therapy, which I am calling here SSI-CBT (WD), is, as I have said, based on the ideas of Albert Ellis, the creator of Rational Emotive Behaviour Therapy (REBT). In this approach to CBT, it is hypothesised that emotional and behavioural problems are underpinned by a set of rigid and extreme attitudes

(Dryden, 2021e), and I am guided by this theoretical point while assessing cognitions at 'B'.

Having pointed out the differences among some of the major CBT approaches, it is important to note the following. When you are practising SSI-CBT in general, and when you are assessing cognition in particular, it is important that you develop a flexible and pluralistic mindset and approach. In my case, while my thinking is influenced by the view that rigid and extreme attitudes underpin clients' emotional and behavioural problems, if a particular client does not accept this view and resonates more, for example, with the ACT position that it is their struggle with their dysfunctional cognitions that is at the root of their nominated problem, then I will proceed on this basis. This is because I would not have the time in SSI-CBT to devote to discussing the merits and de-merits of both positions. In addition, my view is that in SSI-CBT, and I suspect in other approaches to SST too, quickly developing and maintaining an effective working alliance is a crucial idea. This means, in this context, going along with the client's perspective on the relationship between cognition and the person's nominated problem (see Chapters 3 and 7).

Position on case formulation

A case formulation approach to CBT differs from problem assessment in CBT. In the former, a set of mechanisms is put forward to account for the problems that the client is seeking help with, while in the latter each issue is understood on its own merits. In ongoing CBT, the therapist may wish to do a complete case formulation before intervening. In SSI-CBT, there is insufficient time to do this. However, in SSI-CBT, the therapist does have to work with both the specific and the general aspects of the client's nominated problem. Too much emphasis on the particular may mean that the therapist will not discover more general mechanisms that could affect the maintenance of the specific problem if not addressed.

Conversely, too much emphasis on the general may mean that the therapist is unable to help the client sufficiently with their nominated problem.

My approach is that in SSI-CBT, when I have done an assessment of the client's nominated problem and I need to understand this problem from a broader perspective, I will enquire about some of the following factors when indicated:

- How general the client's difficulty is with the adversity at 'A' so that I can suggest ways in which the client can generalise their learning from the adversity in the nominated problem to similar adversities
- Ways in which the client tries to avoid the problem
- Ways in which the client acts to keep themself safe
- Ways in which the client attempts to eliminate experience
- Ways in which the client may try to make themselves feel better
- The client's problematic usage of alcohol, food and drink
- The client's reaction to their nominated problem
- Ways in which the client may overcompensate for having the problem
- Any advantages the client sees to having the problem
- How the client involves other people in their nominated problem
- What the person may lose by achieving their goal

How much case formulation you can do will, as I have said, vary from client to client and how much time you have at your disposal. However, let me reiterate that you cannot do a full case formulation before intervening in SSI-CBT. There is insufficient time to do this.[1]

In this chapter, I have discussed assessing the nominated problem and the importance of identifying the 'B' in the 'ABC' framework. I made the point that different CBT therapists assess 'B' in different ways. I also discussed that while you do not have the time to carry out a full case formulation in SSI-CBT, you can draw upon salient aspects of such a formulation while helping the person with their nominated problem. In the next chapter, I will discuss the assumption that you can identify and work with a central mechanism in SSI-CBT.

Note

1   However, see Jenkins (2020) for a different view on this issue.

11

In SSI-CBT, it is possible to help clients identify and deal with a central mechanism responsible for the existence of their problems

The importance of finding and working with a central mechanism

One of the challenges of single-session therapy is for you to ensure that you help your client take away with them something meaningful in the sense of effectively addressing their nominated problem and moving towards their goal. However, it would be best if you were concerned that what the client takes away with them has long-lasting results. The chances of doing this are enhanced when the client is helped to identify and deal with what I call a central mechanism responsible for their nominated problem. Given the emphasis in SSI-CBT on cognitive and behavioural factors, this central mechanism is likely to be cognitive and have behavioural referents in that it explains why the client acts in the way they do when they are in 'problem' mode. There also needs to be some plausible alternative in cognitive meaning for the client. This needs to suggest alternative and more constructive behaviours that are goal-oriented. Here is an example from my practice of SSI-CBT (WD).

> Barry sought SSI-CBT from me for help with his exam anxiety. What he feared most about examinations was not being able to think clearly and eventually going blank. He also had a similar fear in social situations and would often avoid

DOI: 10.4324/9781003214557-13

people with whom he believed that this would happen. These people would generally be women to whom he was attracted. Although he selected his exam anxiety as his nominated problem, the generic nature of his threat, i.e. his mind going blank, suggested a central mechanism. I thought that if I could promote a shift in how he thought about his mind going blank in the exam arena, I could perhaps help him. The central mechanism responsible for his problem in both arenas was that his mind going blank meant to him that he was an idiot, and this he had to hide from himself and others. The exam arena involved him overpreparing, and in the social arena it involved him avoiding talking to attractive women. As the central mechanism, i.e. 'I am an idiot', suggested alternative meaning systems, this self-evaluation became the focus for examination and change in the session. As we did this, alternative behaviours indicated by the new meaning system (in Barry's case, 'going blank is human and I don't have to hide this') became apparent.

To give yourself the best chance of identifying and thence dealing with a central mechanism, you need to focus on the central core of the client's nominated problem and help the client do the same. You may need to interrupt your client to help them stay focused, and I recommend that you explain in advance that you might have to do this and you seek your client's permission to do so.

The central mechanism in SSI-CBT (WD): an example of theory-driven therapy and open-mindedness

In this section, I will show how I make use of REBT theory in helping clients to identify and deal with a central mechanism in my approach to SSI-CBT that I call SSI-CBT (WD). In my view, REBT theory lends itself to single-session therapy as it advances the idea that people bring their desires to adversities and when they keep these desires flexible (known as a flexible attitude), they handle these adversities constructively. But, on the other hand, when they make these desires rigid (known as a rigid attitude), they disturb themselves and thus don't handle the adversities well (Dryden, 2021e). Therefore, my therapeutic task is to encourage my client to acknowledge their desire with respect to the adversity and keep it flexible.

REBT theory additionally argues that if the person holds a flexible attitude towards an adversity, then they will also tend to hold one or more of three non-extreme attitudes which underpin their constructive handling of the adversity: a non-awfulising attitude (e.g. 'This adversity is bad, but not awful'), a bearability attitude (e.g. 'It is a struggle for me to bear this adversity, but I can bear it, it is worth it to me to do so, I am willing to do so and I am going to do so') and an unconditional acceptance attitude towards self, others or the world (e.g. 'It's bad that this adversity happened, but I am/you are/the world is not bad, but a complex mixture of good, bad and neutral and I can accept myself/you/the world accordingly'). On the other hand, if the person holds a rigid attitude, then they will also tend to hold one or more of three extreme attitudes which underpin their unconstructive response to the adversity: an awfulising attitude (e.g. 'This adversity is bad, and therefore it is awful'), an unbearability attitude (e.g. 'This adversity is a struggle to bear, and therefore I can't bear it') and a devaluation attitude towards self, others or the world (e.g. 'It's bad that this adversity happened and therefore I am/you are/the world is bad'). My therapeutic task here is to help my client acknowledge the evaluation of badness, struggle, and the negative part evaluation respectively where relevant and to keep these attitudes non-extreme.

The final part of REBT theory that is relevant here, and one that has been mentioned in passing above, is the following. When a person holds a set of flexible and non-extreme attitudes towards an adversity, they will tend to experience healthy negative emotions with respect to it, act constructively towards it, and subsequently think in balanced ways. Conversely, when a person holds a set of rigid and extreme attitudes towards the same adversity, they will tend to experience unhealthy negative emotions about it, act unconstructively towards it, and subsequently think in highly distorted ways.

This theory can be summarised in Table 11.1.

Table 11.1 REBT's theory used to help clients identify and deal with their central mechanisms: rigid and extreme attitudes vs flexible and non-extreme attitudes

Rigid Attitudes 'Prefer + Demand Asserted'	Flexible Attitudes 'Prefer + Demand Negated'
↓	↓
Extreme Attitudes	**Non-extreme Attitudes**
• Awfulising Attitudes 'It is Bad + Awful Asserted'	• Non-awfulising Attitudes 'It is Bad + Awful Negated'
• Unbearability Attitudes 'Struggle + Unbearability Asserted'	• Bearability Attitudes 'Struggle + Bearability Asserted + Worth it + Willingness + Going To'
• Devaluation Attitudes 'It is Bad + I/You/World is Bad'	• Unconditional Acceptance Attitudes 'It is Bad + I/You/World is Not Bad + Complex/Fallible

A case example of SSI-CBT (WD)

Let me illustrate how I used REBT theory in my single-session work with Susan.

Sarah was a student and was procrastinating on several university projects and sought SSI-CBT for this issue. As she put it, her goal was to overcome her procrastination and get down to work because doing so would help her get good grades and a good degree. I encouraged Sarah to focus on her central mechanism by asking her what conditions she believed she needed before working on these projects. She replied that before she got down to work, she needed (1) to feel motivated and (2) to know that she would get a good grade. If she had that motivation and were confident that she would get at least a 'B', she would get down to work. Sarah's response to this situation was to try to psych herself up and convince herself that she would get a good grade, strategies that worked only in the very short term.

The 'ABC' assessment that we developed was as follows:

'A' = Lack of motivation, not certain that I will get a good grade
'B' = I must feel motivated and know that I will get a good grade
'C' = Procrastination

My therapeutic task was to help Sarah grasp that her desires for pre-work motivation and outcome confidence were perfectly fine. If she kept her desires for these conditions flexible, she would start work in their absence because she had good reason. Once she accepted this, we looked for a reminder of this central mechanism that would be inspirational and prompt action. Sarah's goal-oriented 'ABC' was as follows:

'A' = Lack of motivation, not sure that I will get a good grade
'B' = It would be good if I felt motivated to do my work and if I knew that I would get a good grade, but I do not need to have my desires met
'C' = Start working

When helping clients to identify a central mechanism in SSI-CBT, it is important to be guided by theory, for as Kurt Lewin (1951) famously noted: 'There is nothing so practical as a good theory.' Thus, I have outlined how REBT theory guides my practice in helping clients in SSI-CBT (WD) to identify and deal with a central mechanism. However, another equally important principle guides my practice in single-session work: if a client does not find REBT theory helpful, then I will not continue to employ it. Instead, I will be open-minded and be guided by the client's view of the central mechanism and use this. In this way, my open-mindedness will preserve the working alliance between myself and my client in the views domain (see Chapter 3).

In this chapter, I discussed the importance of helping your client, if possible, to identify and work with a central mechanism that explains the existence of their problem. In the next chapter, I will consider the assumption made in SSI-CBT that the client's initial reaction to an adversity is not as important as how they respond to that reaction.

12

The client's subsequent responses to their first reaction are often more important than the first reaction itself

Introduction

When people come for therapy, whether single-session therapy or ongoing therapy, they often want to eliminate their problems and the dysfunctional processes involved in these problems. ACT practitioners often point out that our responses to these processes are the problem rather than the processes themselves. Therefore, they would agree that the person's subsequent responses to their first reaction are more important than the first reaction in determining whether or not they have problems.

A note on terminology

Please note that, in this chapter and elsewhere, I refer to the client's initial response to an adversity as a 'reaction' and their subsequent responses to this reaction as 'responses'. I make this distinction because the client's initial reaction to the adversity is often automatic, while their following responses have the more significant potential to be considered.

DOI: 10.4324/9781003214557-14

Subsequent responses to the first reaction:
1. Problematic cognitions

Let's take the example of a person who fails their driving test and gets depressed and reports having the thought/belief: 'I'm a failure.' This thought/belief may be regarded as the person's initial reaction to the adversity of failing the test. Acceptance and mindfulness-based therapists would encourage the person to notice and accept this thought and its associated feeling and get on with the business of value-based living. This noticing, accepting and taking action would be regarded as their subsequent responses to the first reaction: 'I'm a failure.'

CBT therapists who think that helping people to modify their dysfunctional cognitive processes does have value also hold that the person's subsequent responses to their first reaction are more critical than this initial reaction in determining whether or not they have problems. In our example, such therapists would also see the thought/belief 'I'm a failure' as the client's first reaction. However, they would encourage the person to examine this thought for its practical value and empirical status. Some might even encourage the person to question the logic in such a thought/belief in response to failing the driving test. This examination or questioning process and whatever constructive behaviour flows from it would be regarded by such modification-based CBT therapists as the person's subsequent responses to their first reaction: 'I'm a failure.'

Now, the client's subsequent responses to their first reaction can be for better or for worse. Let's begin with the situation where they are for the better. In the first scenario in the above example, if the client puts the acceptance and mindfulness-based CBT therapist's suggestion into practice and notices, accepts and acts, these responses will tend to be constructive. In the second scenario, if the person implements the modification-based CBT therapist's suggestion and examines and questions their thought/belief that they are a failure and acts on whatever more functional thought/

belief they come up with, these subsequent responses will tend to be constructive.

Now let's see what happens when the person's subsequent responses to their first reaction are for the worse. First, there are several ways in which the person's responses to the thought/belief 'I'm a failure' can be unconstructive. Here are a few examples:

- The person can regard the thought/belief as true with the result that they decide that there is no point in trying to learn to drive anymore and thus they do not sign up for any more lessons
- The person regards that having the thought 'I am a failure' proves that there is something wrong with them and feels ashamed for having the thought
- The person can see that the thought/belief 'I am a failure' helps explain their depression about failing the driving test and so endeavours to respond to it so that they disbelieve it entirely. When the thought/belief returns, they consider CBT to have failed or that they are a failure for still having the thought/belief
- The person regards that the best way to deal with the thought/belief 'I'm a failure' is to distract themself from it. Unfortunately, while they may help themself in the very short term, such distraction results in the long-term maintenance of their depression since its cognitive root still has an impact
- The person tries not to think the thought/belief 'I'm a failure' with the result that they think it more frequently, given that thought suppression tends to increase thought frequency (Wegner, 1989)

These points are summarised in Table 12.1.

So far, I have discussed how a person's subsequent responses to a problematic cognition can have either a constructive or an unconstructive impact on that person's well-being. In doing so, I demonstrated my point that it is not the person's initial reaction to an adversity that is important but their subsequent responses to that first response.

Table 12.1 A range of subsequent responses to the person's first reaction to an adversity

Adversity	*First reaction*	*Subsequent responses*	*Impact on well-being*
Fails driving test	'I'm a failure'	Accept, notice and act	Constructive
Fails driving test	'I'm a failure'	Examine thought and act on new thought	Constructive
Fails driving test	'I'm a failure'	Accept as true	Unconstructive
Fails driving test	'I'm a failure'	Shame-based self-criticism	Unconstructive
Fails driving test	'I'm a failure'	Question thought until eliminated; self-criticism when this fails	Unconstructive
Fails driving test	'I'm a failure'	Distraction	Unconstructive
Fails driving test	'I'm a failure'	Thought suppression	Unconstructive

Subsequent responses to the first reaction: 2. Problematic urges

The concept of distinguishing initial reactions and subsequent responses is particularly appropriate when considering helping clients who struggle with dealing with urges or action tendencies. Often people hold the view that if they experience an urge to do something that brings them immediate relief or satisfaction/ pleasure, that is the end of the story. Thus, they are doomed to act on that urge. For these people, the solution to their problem is not to experience that urge. This involves them avoiding situations in which they will likely experience the urge. When they can't avoid the situation, they are likely to do what is shown in Table 12.2.

Table 12.2 First reaction and subsequent response when the client is unable to avoid a situation in which the urge is experienced and acted upon

Adversity	First reaction	Subsequent responses	Impact on well-being
Exposure to situation in which the urge is likely to be experienced	Urge to engage in self-defeating behaviour	Act on the urge	Unconstructive

The therapeutic task here is to help clients see that experiencing an urge to engage in activity that may bring short-term relief or satisfaction/pleasure but which is self-defeating in the longer term is not in itself the problem. It is how clients respond to the urge. Acceptance and mindfulness-based CBT therapists will again encourage clients to notice the impulse, accept it and act in valued ways even though they may still be experiencing the urge. Modification-based CBT therapists will help clients to develop healthy cognitive responses to urges. My practice here is to help clients understand that while it might be preferable for them not to experience the urge in question, that does not mean that they must not experience it, and while they might want to act on it, they don't have to do so. Quite often, a combination of these approaches can be helpful. These two approaches are presented in graphic form in Table 12.3.

SSI-CBT therapists might use such graphics to help clients see what they are doing with respect to their first reactions and how they could respond more constructively to them.

Table 12.3 Two approaches to subsequent constructive responses to the client's first reaction to an adversity

Adversity	First reaction	Subsequent responses	Impact on well-being
Exposure to situation in which the urge is likely to be experienced	Urge to engage in self-defeating behaviour	Notice, accept and act according to values	Constructive
Exposure to situation in which the urge is likely to be experienced	Urge to engage in self-defeating behaviour	Develop healthy cognitions about urge and act according to values	Constructive

In this chapter, I discussed the point that, as an SSI-CBT therapist, you would do better to help your client deal with their subsequent responses to their initial reaction to an adversity rather than help them deal with the initial reaction itself. In the next chapter, I will discuss the importance of drawing on a range of client variables during the SSI-CBT process.

13

It is important to draw upon a range of client variables in SSI-CBT

Introduction

While the outcome of SSI-CBT does depend, to some degree, on what you as the therapist bring to the table, as important, or some would say more important, is what the client brings to the table. While your skills as a therapist are vital, and much of this book is about what you can do to maximise the chances that the client gets the most out of the process, the most skilful SSI-CBT therapists will fail if they don't help their clients to bring the best of themselves to this therapy. Putting these points together, it is possible to argue that your most important skill in SSI-CBT is to help the client use the best of what they have during this process.

In this chapter, I will discuss some of the most important client variables which will maximise the chances that the client will get the most out of the process if used.

Client strengths and values

While CBT has most frequently been employed to help people identify and deal with problems or weaknesses, it can be utilised to identify and capitalise on clients' strengths. Indeed, Padesky and Mooney (2012) have outlined a four-stage strengths-based CBT model to promote resilience, although they argue that it can be employed to foster other qualities as well. But what is strength? Jones-Smith (2014: 13) says that 'strength may be defined as that

DOI: 10.4324/9781003214557-15

which helps a person to cope with life or that which makes life more fulfilling for one and others'. While several people have provided lists of strengths that could theoretically be used to identify those that clients can employ in SSI-CBT (e.g. Buckingham and Clifton, 2014), my approach focuses on what the client thinks their strengths are that might help them get the most out of SSI-CBT.

SSI-CBT also involves you helping the client to identify and utilise their values. Examples of such values include open-mindedness, honesty, loyalty and dependability. You might be thinking about what the difference is between strengths and values. For me, values give direction to a person's goals, while the person draws on their strengths to help them to achieve these goals. As such, both a client's strengths and their values are precious resources in SST.

Helpful people

It is often useful for the client to remember times when someone helped them in their lives. If this was in an area similar to their nominated problem, then so much the better. It is beneficial to discover what the person did that was helpful, as this may help you, as a therapist, tailor your interventions based on this knowledge. In addition, it is useful to find out how the client used the help provided by the other person. Care should be taken to help the client understand that it is what *they* did in response to the assistance provided by the other person that made the difference rather than the help itself. In addition, you should make a note of what the client did to help themself and resolve to capitalise on this later in the process.

A memorable occasion of self-help

It is also useful to have the client focus on a memorable occasion when they helped themself and identify what they did that was helpful. This is not only to help them see that they can turn to themself for help but also perhaps to determine if they can apply what they did on that occasion to their current nominated problem.

Helpful principles

I remember my mother saying to me at various points in my life the following: 'Son, if you don't ask, you don't get.' I took this to mean that if I don't take the initiative in life, then life won't give me what I am seeking. Therefore, I need to 'go for it'. Later on, I amended my mother's principle as follows: 'If you don't ask, you don't get, but asking does not guarantee getting.' I added the latter phrase to remind myself that there is no universal law that decrees that I must get what I want or that it must be given to me just because I am going for it. This revised principle has helped me in two ways. First, it has helped me go for things that I wanted but didn't think I could get, and, second, it has helped me deal with situations when I went for something but did not get it.

For the purposes of SSI-CBT, a good helping principle has the following characteristics: (1) it can be expressed in a concise, memorable way; (2) it guides action and (3) it promotes coping, preferably in the face of adversity. As you can see, my revised principle, 'If you don't ask, you don't get, but asking does not guarantee getting', does all three. If clients struggle to grasp what I mean by 'principle', then I happily share with them both the example I have just presented and the characteristics that a good principle for the purposes of SSI-CBT should ideally have.

When a client identifies with at least one such principle, it is good practice to note it and be on the alert for opportunities to use it later to help the client help themself.

Role models

It is useful to discover who the client considers good role models. These should preferably be people who, if brought to mind, might inspire the person to deal effectively with their nominated problem and work towards their goal. While a good role model does not have to be someone that the person knows personally, it is best if that person can inspire the client despite being fallible. For example, the response you do not want to evoke is: 'I really admire X, but I can't ever imagine being able to do what they have done.' Instead, the client should have the idea: 'Well, they did it, and so can I.'

The most successful role models are people whom the client is very familiar with, looks up to and knows are on their side – someone like a parent, grandparent, another relative, a good friend or a teacher. However, it is best not to rule anyone out if they can inspire the client to deal effectively with their nominated problem.

Discover how the client best learns

It would help if you discovered how your client learns best with particular reference to their nominated problem. While there are several formal ways to assess a person's learning style, the reliability and validity of these measures are questionable (Pashler, McDaniel, Rohrer & Bjork, 2008). However, Pashler and colleagues (2008) did find that, if asked, people will say how they like information presented to them, and I have found that, when asked in SSI-CBT, clients can articulate how they prefer to learn best when it comes to addressing personal problems. So, I recommend that you do this and use the information provided to tailor your interventions accordingly so that your clients can get the most out of the process.

Discover relevant external resources

Although strictly speaking not a client variable, it is helpful to use resources external to the client when helping them develop and plan to implement a solution.

Examples of such resources may be as follows:

- People known to the client who may be useful in some way in helping the client solve their problem
- People not known by the client but whom the client might consult for help
- Organisations that may be useful to the client in their problem-solving efforts and
- Internet sites and 'apps' that might provide useful problem-solving information

This chapter discussed salient client variables that you can help the client draw upon during SSI-CBT. In the following chapter, I will discuss the client characteristics that are helpful in the SSI-CBT process.

14

Helpful client characteristics for SSI-CBT

In this chapter, I will consider the question of what are helpful client characteristics for SSI-CBT. While there are other such characteristics, I will list ten here that I think the most important. While the absence of these characteristics should not be a barrier to the person accessing SSI-CBT, their presence improves the chances that the client will benefit from the process. The more these are present, the greater the likelihood of benefit. Your task as an SSI-CBT is to help your clients to actualise these characteristics whenever possible.

Ready to take care of business now

This is perhaps the most critical client characteristic in that it shows that the client is prepared to work quickly and do what is necessary to solve the problem in the shortest possible time. Human beings can achieve much in a very short period if they demonstrate this readiness. Recall the case of Vera, discussed in Chapter 5. After many months of half-hearted engagement in therapy designed to help her address her elevator phobia, Vera had to deal with this problem in a short time to save her job. An environmental change led her to become ready to take care of business now with excellent results. The questions for you in SSI-CBT are: (1) 'Is my client ready to take care of business now?' And if not, (2) 'How can I promote such readiness?'

DOI: 10.4324/9781003214557-16

Prepared to be as actively engaged as possible in the process

I mentioned in Chapter 3 that it is vital in SSI-CBT for you to take an active role in the process and encourage the client to be as actively engaged as possible. If your client takes a passive, 'feed me' stance in SSI-CBT, it is unlikely that they will get many benefits from the process. So, you need to take every opportunity to promote active client engagement. The use of focused open-ended questions is one example of how you can do this.

Open to your ideas as therapist and be able to be open with you

The success of SSI-CBT depends on a good blend of what you bring to the process as a therapist and what the client brings to the process. For your client to get the most out of what you have to offer, they need to be open to your ideas about factors that determine their nominated problem and what they can do to promote change. But however important that client open-mindedness is, it is equally important for your client to be open with you. In my view, your job as an SSI-CBT therapist is to promote a therapeutic climate where the client can say, 'I don't understand (what you are saying)', 'I don't know (the answer to your question)' and 'I don't agree with you'. The last is particularly important. If the client does not feel able to disagree with you, they will comply with you but will not internalise any change principles. Compliance will only last as long as you, as a therapist, are present, whereas internalisation will work in the long term because the client has made the principle their own. So, it would help if you fostered an atmosphere where the client feels free to speak their mind and, in particular, to disagree with you.

Can focus and clearly and specifically articulate their nominated problem and related goal

SSI-CBT can often be a very focused approach to helping clients achieve their goals in the shortest time possible. For this to be done, your client needs to focus quickly on their nominated problem and what they want to get out of their work with you. While such focus is a key ingredient, the client must also be able to articulate clearly and precisely the nature of their nominated problem, the factors that help determine the issue and what their goal is concerning the issue. Both clarity and specificity are important here.

Given that it is vital for your client to demonstrate focus, clarity and specificity, you as their therapist should encourage these client characteristics to come to the fore throughout the SSI-CBT process. However, suppose it becomes apparent during the single session that the client cannot demonstrate these characteristics sufficiently to enable you to help them solve their problem. In that case, they will probably need further help, should they choose to access it.

Realistic about what can be achieved in SSI-CBT

I mentioned in Chapter 6 that there is a concept known as 'quantum change' that was introduced to the literature by Miller and C'de Baca (2001). They define such rapid and dramatic change as 'a vivid, surprising, benevolent and enduring personal transformation' (Miller and C'de Baca, 2001: 4). While it is unlikely that such transformation will occur in planned SSI-CBT, it is not inconceivable that this might happen. More likely, however, is that the client makes a change that will help them to get unstuck from a pattern of thinking, feeling and behaviour that has resulted in the perpetuation of a personal problem from which they have not been able to free themself. In my view, clients who have realistic ideas of what they can get from SSI-CBT will achieve more than those expecting a quantum change. Indeed, I would hypothesise that if quantum change does occur in SSI-CBT, it will be achieved by clients who have realistic expectations of the process rather than those actively seeking quantum change.

Miller and C'de Baca (2001) cite two well-known fictional characters as examples of quantum change – George Bailey from the Frank Capra film *It's a Wonderful Life* and Ebenezer Scrooge from the Charles Dickens tale *A Christmas Carol.* Both did not seek quantum change; indeed, neither sought change at all. It may be said, with due poetic licence, that quantum change sought them! However, they did make use of the opportunity. My view, then, is that your primary role as an SSI-CBT therapist is to help your client get the most out of the opportunity that this therapeutic approach provides rather than trying actively to promote quantum change. If such change does occur in SSI-CBT, it will happen for reasons only tangentially related to what you, as a therapist, did.

Prepared to put into practice what they learn from their contact with you

One of the most robust findings from the literature on CBT is that clients who put into practice what they learn in sessions get more out of the process than people who do not put their learning into practice. Thus, it would be wise to ask your client at the very first contact with you (see Chapter 18) whether or not they are prepared to put what they learn from their SSI-CBT session into practice in their everyday life. However, just because a client says at the outset that they are not prepared to act on their learning, it may happen that during the session they change their mind. Thus, do not exclude the person from accessing SSI-CBT in this circumstance.

It would help if you capitalised on your client's preparedness to practise what they learn by helping them to develop a solution to their nominated problem and a plan to implement this. While this is not strictly speaking a 'homework assignment', it is helpful to discuss how the client will specifically begin their implementation programme.

Can move with relative ease from the specific to the general and back again

While the ability to focus and specify problems and goals is a vital client characteristic in SSI-CBT, it is also important for a person to move with ease from the specific to the general and back again. Too detailed a focus will result in the person making only a very localised change in their life. On the other hand, too broad a focus will result in the client taking away some general principles that they will find difficult to apply to concrete situations. In my view, the ideal situation in SSI-CBT is for the client to effectively address their nominated problem and understand how general principles relevant to that problem can also be applied to other issues and other appropriate situations. As an SSI-CBT therapist, I am mainly focused on the client's nominated problem but also looking for opportunities to help the client generalise learning to other contexts in that client's life.

Can relate to metaphors, aphorisms, stories and imagery

Most therapy involves the use of words. Because time is at a premium in SSI-CBT, both you and your client need to work quite quickly to make the most of the time available to both of you. Consequently, you will exchange quite a lot of words in your contact with one another. One of your therapeutic tasks is to help your client to create new meaning, which is an instrumental part of the change process in SSI-CBT. While this new meaning will be in the form of words, it needs to be memorable if the client is to implement it in their own life over time. One way of making meaning memorable is to use metaphors (i.e. figures of speech in which a term or phrase is applied to something to which it is not literally applicable to suggest a resemblance), aphorisms (pithy and memorable statements that contain a general truth and an astute observation), stories and imagery. Clients who relate to such media of expression tend to have a more emotionally impactful experience of

SSI-CBT than those who do not relate as well and so may get more out of the process. However, this needs to be tested empirically (see Chapter 26).

Prepared to engage in activities where they can practise solutions in the session

I mentioned emotional impact in the previous section. Another way of increasing such impact with clients is to engage them in activities where they can practise solutions in the session (see Chapter 27). Role-play and chairwork (Kellogg, 2015) are good examples of such activities.

I used role-play with Susan towards the end of our session in which she realised that the best way of dealing with her feelings of depression was to assert herself with her boss, who was making unreasonable demands on her at work. I first helped Susan see that she was playing the role of the helpless victim at work, which helped maintain her depression and did not dissuade her boss from giving her extra work every week. She first decided to stop being a victim and help herself by addressing the issue with her boss. I played her boss and gave her extra work in the role-play, and she asserted herself with me. After a few false starts, she got into the role and stood up to me-as-boss very well. She also developed her own aphorism, 'Victim no more', and resolved to assert herself with her boyfriend and her mother as well as with her boss. At follow-up, she reported better relations with her mother, a workload on a par with her colleagues and a new boyfriend who respected her more than the old one who did not like the new, more assertive, Susan and ended their relationship.

Has a sense of humour

The final helpful client characteristic reflects my personal view and personal preference to inject humour into the SSI-CBT process. For me, the effective use of humour in SSI-CBT enables both you and your client to treat serious issues with a light touch but without trivialising the issues. In doing so, it takes the horror out of the issues and promotes an attitude in the client that they can learn 'to take life seriously but not too seriously', in the words of Albert Ellis. Consequently, I think that clients who do have a sense of humour bring the best out of me as an SSI-CBT therapist, and this encourages me to help them get the best out of the process.

Having considered helpful client characteristics for SSI-CBT, let me conclude the first part of the book by discussing helpful therapist characteristics for SSI-CBT.

Helpful therapist characteristics for SSI-CBT

Not all therapists want to practise SSI-CBT. My view is that, in the same way that clients should not be compelled to have SSI-CBT, therapists should not be obliged to practise it when they don't want to. Therapists also differ in their suitability to practise SSI-CBT. In my view, the following are therapist characteristics that are particularly conducive to its effective practice.

Can tolerate lack of information about clients

A common objection to SSI-CBT comes from CBT therapists who hold that they cannot do therapy without first carrying out a thorough case formulation. Given this position, they argue that the single-session format does not give them enough time to carry out such a case formulation. While there is truth to this position, SSI-CBT therapists say that you can practise SSI-CBT effectively without first having done a case formulation. As I discussed in Chapter 10, it is possible to do *some* formulation work in the time available, which is usually sufficient when devoted to a thorough problem and goal assessment. Thus, it is helpful to tolerate not having as much client information as one would like to be a good SSI-CBT therapist.

DOI: 10.4324/9781003214557-17

Does not need close relationships with clients

Another objection to SSI-CBT comes from therapists who argue that it is necessary to form close relationships with clients to practise therapy effectively. In their view, the SSI-CBT format does not give them sufficient time to do this. SSI-CBT therapists would respond that effective work can be done in SSI-CBT without the development of close therapist–client relationships and that what is more important is developing a good working alliance (see Chapter 3).

Can engage quickly with clients

In SSI-CBT, what is more important than developing a close relationship with clients is to engage with them quickly. You usually do this by focusing very early on their nominated problem and what they want to get out of SSI-CBT. However, by eliciting clients' strengths and other variables that will aid you in helping these clients more effectively, you will engage with them more efficiently because they will be focusing on their positive attributes rather than just their deficits. In addition, quick engagement is facilitated by you showing your clients, by your demeanour and your behaviour, that you are genuinely interested in helping them as quickly as possible.

Can be an authentic chameleon

My friend and colleague the late Arnold Lazarus (1993) introduced the concept of the therapist as an 'authentic chameleon' into the psychotherapy literature. This concept describes a helpful therapist characteristic for SSI-CBT where you show that you can authentically vary your interpersonal style with different clients and can astutely determine which clients would resonate with which style. While SSI-CBT can be practised by therapists who have a standard therapeutic style, my view is that these therapists will be less effective than therapists who are flexible in their interpersonal relating with their clients.

Is flexible and has a pluralistic outlook

As I have already mentioned, SSI-CBT is best regarded as a framework rather than a specific approach and can accommodate different CBT approaches. Therefore, CBT therapists who practise SSI-CBT will bring their way of using CBT to the work, and I exemplify my work, that I refer to as SSI-CBT (WD), throughout this book. However, while effective SSI-CBT therapists will have their own approach, they will be prepared to be flexible and pluralistic in their CBT practice. You can demonstrate flexibility and pluralism in SSI-CBT in the following ways:

- By conceptualising your clients' problems and goals in different ways if your original conceptualisation does not make sense to the client
- By acknowledging that there is no one right way of practising SSI-CBT. You will, therefore, vary your practice with different clients and be prepared to use methods both from other CBT approaches and from approaches from outside CBT when the situation calls for it
- By bringing a both/and perspective to the work rather than an either/or perspective
- By drawing on clients' resources and encouraging clients to use these in the session and beyond (see Chapter 13)
- By involving clients fully at every stage of the process

Can think quickly on their feet

Some therapists prefer to take their time in therapy and to reflect in a leisurely manner about the process as it unfolds. Such therapists would find the practice of SSI-CBT quite challenging because it does require therapists to think quickly on their feet. Therapists who have this cognitive facility and enjoy opportunities to use it tend to make effective SSI-CBT practitioners.

Can help clients focus quickly and collaboratively

In an important respect, the effective practice of SSI-CBT depends on you helping your client to find a meaningful focus for the work. If you cannot find such a focus, then the potency of SSI-CBT as a way of working is significantly diluted. Thus, therapists who can help clients focus, and can do so quickly without rushing them, tend to do very well in SSI-CBT. This notion of finding a focus quickly but without rushing the client is crucial.

Some therapists can quickly focus but do not bring the client along with them at the client's speed. Instead, the work has the quality of the client being dragged along too quickly. The result will often be that the client will not fully process what is on offer and will not, therefore, get very much from the process. Thus, the therapist must help the client focus quickly but do so collaboratively. Here the work has the quality of two people working together in a focused manner at a pace that suits them both.

Has realistic expectations of SSI-CBT

In Chapters 6 and 14, I mentioned that quantum change, while possible, is unlikely to be experienced by SSI-CBT clients. Much more commonly, SSI-CBT helps clients to free themselves from stuck patterns and get on with their life in a given area. While clients who have realistic expectations from SSI-CBT will tend to get more out of the process than clients who think this approach will help them change more general chronic problems, the same is true of therapists. For you to be an effective SSI-CBT therapist, you will tend to be optimistic but realistic in what you think you can help your clients achieve. By contrast, those therapists who, on the one hand, are pessimistic about what can be achieved or, on the other, are unrealistic about what clients can get out of the process tend not to be effective and are perhaps not suited to be SSI-CBT practitioners.

Can move with relative ease from the specific to the general and back again

In the previous chapter, I mentioned that a vital client characteristic for SSI-CBT is moving quite readily from the specific to the general and vice versa. This is also a key therapist characteristic. If you take an overly specific focus with your client, the effect will be limited for them. Additionally, if you take a general focus with them, they will take away only theoretical learning that they probably won't use in specific situations. Therefore, your central task as an SSI-CBT therapist, in my view, is to take an appropriately specific focus with your client. Although doing so will help them deal effectively with their nominated problem, it will also help them see how they can generalise their learning.

Can use metaphors, aphorisms, stories and imagery and tailor them to the client

Ideally, the process of SSI-CBT should have an emotional impact on clients (see Chapter 26). This may happen in the ordinary course of therapeutic conversation. Still, it may be enhanced if you employ a suitable metaphor, a pithy and relevant aphorism, an appropriate story, or an image developed either by the client themself or suggested by you. These methods help encapsulate the main learning point for the client in a highly memorable way and tend to be remembered both for the methods and the learning point well after SSI-CBT has finished. Therapists who can readily employ such techniques may be more suited to the practice of SSI-CBT than therapists who rely only on straightforward verbal dialogue without the use of such procedures.

This concludes Part I of the book, in which I presented the theoretical underpinnings of SSI-CBT. In Part II, I will focus much more pointedly on its practice. In doing so, I will demonstrate how the process of SSI-CBT unfolds by following one client's progress from start to finish.

Part II

PRACTICE

16

Good practice in SSI-CBT

Before I discuss, in detail, the process of SSI-CBT, let me outline what I consider to be good practice in SSI-CBT. These are general points of practice that will facilitate the process and outcome of SSI-CBT if implemented. In what follows, I will briefly review a number of broad ways of intervening that characterise good practice in SSI-CBT.

Engage the client quickly

SSI-CBT is an approach to helping people that involves you using time very efficiently (see Chapter 2). There is no time to waste on conversation that is not focused on the task at hand. Thus, engaging the client quickly is critical to getting the process off on the right foot.

Develop rapport through the work

In SSI-CBT, there is no distinction made between rapport building and getting the work done. Indeed, it is argued that the best way of developing rapport with clients is to show them that you are very keen to help them address their problems and goals as quickly as possible and to get down to the business of doing so.

DOI: 10.4324/9781003214557-19

Be clear about why you are both here and what you both can and cannot do

If the client is going to get the most out of SSI-CBT, it is important that you and they both share the same ideas about the purpose of your contact and what can be realistically achieved from this contact. It is your responsibility as a therapist to ensure that both of you share the same views on this matter. As mentioned in Chapter 2, the principle of transparency means that you need to be clear about what you can and cannot do in SSI-CBT.

Be active-directive

In general, CBT is a therapeutic tradition where you are called upon to adopt an active-directive therapeutic style. It is no different in SSI-CBT where, from the outset, you need to be active in directing yourself and your client to the latter's nominated problem and what they want to get out of such discussion. However, you need to ensure that you also encourage your client to be active in the process of adopting an active-directive style. If the client is rendered passive by your activity, then they will probably derive little benefit from SSI-CBT.

Sometimes, however, a client may wish to explore an issue or express their feelings about an issue. You may want to vary your therapeutic style to meet your client's helping preferences in such circumstances.

Be focused and help the client stay focused

Concerning the issue of focus, you have two important tasks to perform. First, you need to help the client identify a focus for the work – e.g. a problem they are stuck with for which they would like help to get unstuck – and, second, you need to help the client stay focused on this nominated issue. Clients vary in their ability to stay with a focus once it has been co-created, and it is your job to help them do this by your questions and, if necessary, by interrupting the client and re-directing them back to the focus. As I have already mentioned, but it is a point worth repeating, it is best if (1) you explain in advance that you may need to interrupt the client if they move away from the agreed focus and (2) you ask for permission to do so.

It should also be clear that you need to guard against moving away from the agreed focus yourself.

Assess the client's nominated problem with an imminent, future example if possible

Once you have elicited the problem from the client's perspective, the next stage is for you to assess it. In general, at the outset, CBT therapists will usually consider examples of problems, either those that are presently occurring in the client's life or that have occurred in their recent past. In SSI-CBT, this may also be done, but I suggest that, if possible, you assess an imminent, future example of your client's problem. The rationale for this is as follows.

The goal of SSI-CBT is to help the client quickly set a goal and take away a new perspective that will allow them to move on with their lives. Thus, both you and your client are facing forwards, as it were. When you assess a past or current example of the client's problem, you face backwards or sideways. When it comes to implementing the solution, you have helped the client select the sideways and backwards facing therapeutic dyad and then have to adjust their position and face forward. In contrast, the forward-facing pair are already facing in that direction. This shows that starting with assessing the nominated problem with an imminent, future example, if possible, is the more efficient strategy since putting new learning into practice will be done in the setting that has already been assessed.

In explaining this rationale to clients, I may say something like:

'In my view, the limited time that we have with one another is best spent seeing how you can best implement what you may learn here in your life going forward. Given this, the more we can focus on an imminent, future example of your problem, the more likely it is that you will apply what you learn here to those situations when you face them. What is your response to this strategy?'

If the client disagrees with this strategy, we can use that disagreement as a springboard to agree on a way forward. Here, as elsewhere, preserving the alliance is more important than pushing the client into working with a strategy to which they are opposed, no matter how much this strategy might represent good practice in SSI-CBT.

Elicit the client's goals and keep focused on this

CBT therapists, in general, are goal-oriented, and this is even more the case in SSI-CBT. As discussed in Chapter 2, you will help the client set a session goal and a problem-related goal. Concerning the latter, once a goal has been identified, it is good practice for you to help the client keep your joint focus on this goal, whether this be a goal in the face of adversity (see Chapter 4) or not. I will discuss working with goals in SSI-CBT in greater detail in Chapter 23.

Ensure that this goal-oriented focus is underpinned by a value if possible

As an SSI-CBT therapist, you will be aware of the limited time you have with your client, and therefore you need to discover ways of increasing the chances that what your client achieves from the process endures. One way of doing this is to help the client find a strong value that might underpin their goal since goals underpinned by values are more likely to be achieved than goals that aren't (Eccles and Wigfield, 2002). I will discuss this issue further in Chapter 23.

Ask what the client is prepared to sacrifice to achieve their goal

SSI-CBT is based on a blend of optimism and realism. It is optimistic in the sense that it holds that clients can be helped to address their nominated problems effectively in a single session when proper preparations have been made for that session. It is realistic because it acknowledges that clients are more likely to achieve their goals if they are prepared to make sacrifices to achieve them. Therefore, it is good practice for you to raise this issue with your clients at the appropriate time.

Whenever practicable, explain what you plan to do in SSI-CBT and seek the client's permission to proceed

In my view, it is good practice in SSI-CBT to explain, whenever practicable, what you plan to do so that the client understands it and is entirely on board with it. There is no time for you to explain everything you plan to do, and neither would it be wise for you to do so, as this would interfere with what you are both there for – helping the client move on with their lives as quickly as possible. However, whenever you are likely to adopt a strategy that the client might not realistically expect or may struggle to understand, then it is wise to offer a rationale and ask for permission to proceed. Here are a few additional examples of strategies where you might usefully explain what you plan to do and seek permission to proceed:

- Discussing a specific example of the client's nominated problem
- Examining the client's problematic cognitions
- Interrupting the client if they go off track
- Offering a relevant piece of therapist self-disclosure

Encourage the client to be as specific as possible, but be mindful of opportunities for generalisation

I have mentioned several times already the importance of specificity in SSI-CBT. Working with such specificity has several advantages: (1) it helps both you and your client understand more clearly the factors that explain why the problem persists; (2) it is more likely to engage the client emotionally with the process than will keeping things general; and (3) it gives both you and your client a clear vision of what the latter might change to achieve their goals.

However, it is also crucial for you to be mindful of opportunities to help clients generalise their learning. Thus, managing the specific–general continuum and moving flexibly along this continuum in both directions represents good practice in SSI-CBT. Doing so will help the client get as much out of the process as possible.

Identify and make use of the client's strengths

As I discussed in Chapter 13, it is important for you to seek information about many client variables to assist them in getting the most out of the process. One of these variables – client strengths – is especially beneficial. Thus, it is good practice to base SSI-CBT on clients' strengths rather than just focusing on their problems.

Identify the client's previous attempts to solve the nominated problem; capitalise on successful attempts and distance yourself from unsuccessful attempts

The efficient use of time is paramount in SSI-CBT. Therefore, it is vital that you do not waste time trying to help clients in ways that they have already tried and have failed. Thus, it is good practice in SSI-CBT to discover what your client has already done to address their problem and capitalise on things they have tried that yielded some success and to distance yourself from things they have tried that proved unsuccessful.

Identify and be mindful of the client's learning style

As I mentioned in Chapter 13, it is important for you to plan your interventions with your client's learning style in mind. Asking your client how they best learn with respect to their problem is direct and may yield the explicit information you need to help them get the best from SSI-CBT.

Encourage the client to prepare and reflect throughout the process

To encourage your client to get the most out of the SSI-CBT process, it is good practice for you to help them to prepare for different parts of this process and reflect on these different parts.

Encourage the client to prepare

In my practice of SSI-CBT, I encourage my clients to complete a pre-session questionnaire before we have the session (see Table 19.1). I also encourage them to prepare for the follow-up session when we have it. In the pre-session questionnaire, I want the client to think about: (1) the resources that they can bring to the process to achieve whatever their goal is and (2) what they want to achieve from the sessions. For the follow-up, I want them to reflect on two things: (1) what they achieved from the process, and what they did to bring about what they achieved, and (2) what was helpful and unhelpful about the process and what I could have done differently to help them more effectively.

Encourage the client to reflect

It is also my practice to encourage my clients to refrain from turning on their mobile phones and tablets for 30 minutes after the session so that they can reflect on what they have learned from it and how they can apply this learning in their lives with respect to the nominated problem and also to other related areas.

To aid reflection, I also send them on request after the session a copy of the digital voice recording (DVR) that I routinely make of my single sessions and also the transcript of this recording. I encourage them to refer to one or other or both of these materials when they wish to refresh their memory of the work we have done together. I discuss the use of these materials more fully in Chapter 29.

The use of questions in SSI-CBT

Make liberal use of questions

If you have been trained in CBT, you will be comfortable with the idea of asking questions. However, suppose you were initially trained in the humanistic and psychodynamic approaches. In that case, you may have problems with this aspect of SSI-CBT practice since these approaches tend to caution against the liberal use of questions. As asking many questions is the *sine qua non* of SSI-CBT practice, you will need to adjust to this core component of the approach if you are to practise it effectively.

Ensure that the client answers the questions you ask them

In my view, questions in SSI-CBT are like surgical incisions in that they are designed to get to the heart of the matter. Given the vital role that asking questions has in SSI-CBT, it is good practice for you to ensure that the client does answer the questions you have asked them. If they have not answered an important question, then you need to ask it again until the client does answer it. This should be a focused but gentle process and not an interrogation. However, suppose the client continues to struggle to answer the question. In that case, you should drop the question and take a different tack, even if the question is fundamental, as to persist will threaten the working alliance, which should be avoided if possible.

Give the client time to answer your questions

One of the things that experienced SSI-CBT therapists can do is use time effectively without rushing the client. Mesut Özil, who used to play for Arsenal, is a football player who could get the job done while seeming to take his time doing so. In training SSI-CBT therapists, I show video clips of Özil playing to demonstrate what I mean. 'Doing an Özil' has come to mean making sure that the client answers the therapist's questions but giving them time to do so. Thus, making effective use of the time at your disposal without rushing your client is a hallmark of good SSI-CBT practice.

Check out the client's understanding of your substantive points

What is the difference between teaching and learning? Teaching is the input provided by the teacher, while learning is what the learner takes away from the process. I mention this point because it is relevant to SSI-CBT. Thus, if you make a substantive point during the process, ask the client for their understanding of the point made.

Otherwise, you may think that the client understands when they don't. There is no good course without a test!

Identify and respond to the client's doubts, reservations and objections, including those that may be expressed non-verbally

I have mentioned several times already that it is vital that you and your client agree about different facets of the SSI-CBT process. If you do not, then the client won't derive as much benefit from SSI-CBT as they could if you both agreed on these facets. Given this, it is good practice for you to ask the client if they have any doubts, reservations or objections (DROs) about any aspect of the process. Otherwise, the client's DRO(s) will still exist and negatively impact them during the process with detrimental results for the person.

Sometimes the client will indicate non-verbally that they have a DRO about the process. When you notice this, you should check it out with the client and deal with their issue.

Look for ways of making an emotional impact on the client during the session

In CBT, the distinction is made between intellectual insight and emotional insight (Ellis, 1963). By intellectual insight, a theoretical understanding of a salient point is meant. In contrast, emotional insight refers to a deep conviction in the same point that impacts the person's feelings and behaviour. In ongoing CBT, the path from intellectual insight to emotional insight is usually made by the client executing relevant homework assignments over time which are negotiated and reviewed. In SSI-CBT, there is insufficient time to promote this process in this way. Consequently, you need to look for ways to make an emotional impact with the client some time during the session, if possible. While benefit can be derived from

SSI-CBT without such impact, the benefit is enhanced with it, in my experience.

Try to ensure that the client takes one meaningful point from the process and has a plan to implement this point

I have raised the issue several times in this book concerning what can be realistically expected from SSI-CBT. My view on this point is that if you can help the client take one meaningful point from the process with a plan to put this point into practice, you have done a good job. Sometimes, however, when I think that the client has done this, nothing fruitful has occurred for the client. The converse is also true; when I think that the client has not taken anything meaningful from the process, they have derived great benefit. Having said this, it is good practice for therapists to strive to help the client plan to implement that one meaningful point (Keller and Papasan, 2012).

Have the client summarise the session

Because the goal of SSI-CBT is to help the person take something meaningful from the process, it is helpful for you to ensure that the client is clear about what is happening throughout the process. Therefore, periodically, it is good practice to ask the client to summarise what has been covered. The most critical summary is the one that the client makes at the end of the session, as this is the point that will influence what the person puts into practice.

Tie up loose ends

Because the end of the face-to-face session is important, the client should have an opportunity to ask something so that they do not go away confused on some issue. Consequently, it is important that you tie up any loose ends with the client before they leave the session.

Plan for and carry out follow-up

The follow-up phase of SSI-CBT is an integral part of the process, in my view, and thus you need to provide a rationale for it and organise when the follow-up session will take place before the client leaves at the end of the session. So, I suggest that you make a definite time for this contact, which is generally conducted over the telephone between you and the client. It needs to be at a time when the client can talk freely without interruption.

Having outlined good practice in SSI-CBT, in the following chapter I will provide an overview of the process before discussing each part of that process in detail in the rest of the book.

17

An overview of the SSI-CBT process

Before I discuss the process of SSI-CBT in detail, I will first present an overview of this process. Let me be clear at the outset that this process comes from my practice of SSI-CBT, and it may be that other therapists would conceptualise this process somewhat differently.

The process of SSI-CBT, as discussed in this book, involves four stages:

1. The first contact
2. Pre-session preparation
3. The single session
4. The follow-up session

The first contact

A first contact represents the first time that the person seeking help makes contact with you or with the agency where you work. While I will discuss this further in the next chapter, let me say here that the main objective of the first contact is to outline the services on offer so that the person can make an informed decision on whether to access SSI-CBT. If so, arrangements are then made for the person to move to the next stage.

DOI: 10.4324/9781003214557-20

Pre-session preparation

After the initial contact, it is helpful for the person to prepare for the session. I used to do this by a telephone call that lasted between 20 and 30 minutes. Currently, to bring down costs for the person, I usually encourage the person to prepare for the session by completing a pre-session questionnaire (see Table 19.1). Once they have done this, I invite them to send it to me before the session takes place so that I can gain an idea of what the person is seeking from the session. I will discuss the points to cover in this second phase point of contact in Chapter 19.

Not all clients complete a pre-session questionnaire, and, in this case, the work begins in the session.

The session

Before the Covid-19 pandemic, I would do all my single-session work face-to-face, but subsequently I have done it all virtually via an online platform. Apart from the difficulties caused by variable internet connections, I have found that SSI-CBT is just as effective online as face-to-face. The former has made SSI-CBT more accessible to a vast number of people.

I tell clients that my single sessions last *up to* 50 minutes since I want the option to end the session earlier if we have done the work before 50 minutes have elapsed. The impact of the session is compromised if we have done the work that we need to in a shorter period, and then we have to fill in time until 50 minutes have passed.

The first thing I do in the session is refer to the pre-session questionnaire that the client has completed and enquire about any changes that the client may have noticed since they completed the form.

My next task is to help the client create a focus for the session and then identify their nominated problem (i.e. the problem they want to be assisted with), their goal concerning that problem, and their session goal. Problem and goal assessment follows, based on a selected example of the problem.[1]. During this assessment, if all goes well, I help the client develop a working understanding of the model that underpins the assessment. The next stage is for the person to examine the troublesome cognitions that are mainly deemed responsible for the problem and either modify these and plan on acting on the new cognitions or accept the problematic cognitions mindfully and thence act in valued ways – or a combination of the two strategies. This comprises the solution to the client's problem. Throughout this process, I look for ways to make an emotional impact on the client, which may encourage learning and later application.

Then, if relevant and feasible, I encourage the client to rehearse the solution that we have agreed upon in the session (e.g. with role-play or chairwork). After which, I encourage the client to think about how they will implement their learning in their everyday life as soon as possible after the session. I will also see if I can help the client to generalise their learning. At the end of the session, a final summary should be made, preferably by the client and augmented by you, and any loose ends tied up. I then make an appointment for the follow-up session at a date nominated by the client. I tell the client that they are responsible for initiating this last contact, usually by telephone.

One of the features of my practice, SSI-CBT (WD), is that I record the session and offer my client the digital voice recording (DVR) of the session and a typed transcript. Doing so aids client reflection, gives the client something to review after the final session, and provides a valuable bridge between the session and the follow-up session. However, it should be noted that not every SSI-CBT therapist does this.

The follow-up session

Some clients say that knowing that they would have further contact with me as a therapist was a motivation to help them maintain the gains they made from the session. Others welcome the chance to reflect on the process as it serves as a reminder of what was achieved since the session and what can yet be achieved.

Follow-up also enables me to discover what was helpful and not so helpful about my contribution to the process, and thus it aids my development as an SSI-CBT therapist. Finally, if you are working in a service that collects data on intervention effectiveness, follow-up is crucial in finding out just how effective SSI-CBT is with clients who choose to access it. It also yields data on differential effectiveness among therapists.

In this chapter, I have presented a process view of SSI-CBT, mainly as I practise it. In doing so, I outlined four stages of this process. In the chapters that follow, I discuss good practice at each of these stages in further detail and provide illustrations from my work with an SSI-CBT client.

Note

1   See Chapter 16 for a brief discussion of the value of working with an imminent, future example of the nominated problem.

18

The first contact

From an SSI-CBT perspective, the purpose of the first contact between you and the person who has made that contact is for that person to determine whether they want to access SSI-CBT.

How that contact is made will depend upon your working environment. If you work for yourself and take your own phone calls, you will be able to explain to the person who has called you what services you offer, in general, which will include single-session work. If you work in an agency where a receptionist, for example, is the first port of call for potential clients, the agency should ideally train the receptionist to be clear about the services that the agency offers, including single-session therapy.

In what follows, I will assume that you yourself will be the person who will be the first point of contact for your potential client. Whether you have answered the telephone when the person rings or whether you are returning their call, I recommend that you first ascertain whether the person has contacted you specifically for single-session therapy or whether they are requesting some other service. Suppose they have contacted you for single-session therapy specifically. In that case, I suggest that you explain to them what the process involves, including cost, so that they can make an informed decision to proceed. If they have contacted you for some other service, for example ongoing CBT, then you have a choice. You can either offer them an appointment for ongoing work or outline the services you provide to ensure that they know the full range of services and can make an informed decision. Outlining the range of

DOI: 10.4324/9781003214557-21

services that you offer is a good idea, particularly when the person who has called is not sure, at that time, which service may meet their therapeutic needs. In my case, I outline the four services that I offer in my practice: (1) ongoing therapy, (2) single-session therapy, (3) coaching and (4) couples therapy.

In this part of the book, I will be referring to the single-session work that I did with Eugene,[1] a 25-year-old accountant who contacted me for help with anxiety concerning work-related presentations that he was called upon to give as part of his employment. What follows has been taken from the first contact that Eugene and I had.

Eugene:	I was given your number by my sister-in-law, who thought that you might be able to help me.
Windy:	Do you have any idea what particular type of help you are looking for?
Eugene:	Well, I was told that you practise CBT, but I'm not sure other than that.
Windy:	Would it help if I outlined services that I do offer?
Eugene:	Yes.
Windy:	First, I offer ongoing CBT, mainly for people who have either one chronic problem that they have struggled with for many years or a range of issues that they are looking to address. Second, I offer single-session CBT for people who have a particular problem with which they feel stuck but are keen to address as quickly as possible to move on with their lives without being constrained by that problem. Third, I offer coaching for people who don't have any specific or general issues in their lives but feel that they are not getting as much out of their life as they could get either in their personal lives, their work lives or their relationships. Finally, I offer couples therapy

> for people with relationship problems that they want to address together with me as their therapist. Which of these services do you think at the moment best suits you and your situation?

After Eugene had indicated that he thought SSI-CBT was the most relevant service for him, I proceeded with this.

Windy: So, let me explain a little bit more about the single-session therapy process. I will send you a pre-session questionnaire for you to complete. This is an integral part of the process and helps you prepare for the session to get the most from it. I ask you to return the form before the session so that I can read it and prepare for the session as well.

The session lasts up to 50 minutes, and because of the pandemic will take place by Zoom. At the end of the session, I will send you an audio recording of the session for your later review. If you want me to, I will also send you a written transcript of the session. This will cost you extra since I have to pay the person who transcribes the session.

After the session, we will have a follow-up session by telephone at a time decided by you to feed back to me the progress you have made since we spoke and let me know what you thought of the service. Do you have any questions?

The major question people have is about the cost, which I answer and indicate that the fee includes the pre-session questionnaire, the session, the follow-up session and the recording.

A written transcript of the session is extra (as explained above), and if they want to save money, they can do so by not having this. I will discuss the role of the recording and the transcript in Chapter 29. I also inform the person about other practicalities, such as my cancellation policy and the exceptions to absolute confidentiality.

After I have answered all the person's questions and they indicate that they wish to proceed with SSI-CBT, I will make an appointment for the session and send them, by email attachment, the pre-session questionnaire to complete and return before the session.

In this chapter, I discussed how to respond to the person's first contact. In the next chapter, I will discuss the pre-session preparation I ask the person to do before the session.

Note

1 The case of 'Eugene' is a composite case. This means that the work has been drawn from a number of different SSI-CBT cases that I have seen. The exchanges that I report when discussing SSI-CBT with Eugene did not actually take place but are highly representative of the work that I do with clients in my SSI-CBT practice.

19

Pre-session preparation

In my practice of SSI-CBT, I have moved from carrying out a pre-session telephone call to help the person prepare for the session to asking a person to prepare for the session themselves by completing a questionnaire. Such preparation aims to help the person get the most out of the session when they have it. There are several reasons why I have done so. First, it helps keep the costs of SSI-CBT down for the client. Second, doing so promotes client autonomy. Third, while completing a questionnaire, the client can take their time and stop and think about their answers, which would not be possible in a time-limited telephone call.

However, there is a downside to the shift that I have made on this issue. First, when the client completes a questionnaire and writes something that I am not clear about or I want to explore further, I cannot do either of these things. Second, if a client fills out the questionnaire in a cursory manner, there is nothing I can do about this, while during preparation by telephone I can prompt and encourage if the client gives monosyllabic answers.

Table 19.1 presents the pre-session questionnaire that I currently use, and Table 19.2 shows the responses given by Eugene, whose case I present in the book to demonstrate the process of SSI-CBT.

After the person has completed the questionnaire, I request that they send it to me so that I can prepare for the session as well.

In this chapter, I have discussed the importance of the client preparing for the session and provided a copy of the pre-session questionnaire that I currently use.

DOI: 10.4324/9781003214557-22

Table 19.1 Pre-session questionnaire

I invite you to fill in this questionnaire before your single session with me. It is a very important part of the process so please engage with the questions as much as you can. I have found that it helps people to prepare for their session with me so that they can get the most from it. It also helps me to help you as effectively as I can. Please return it by email attachment before our session. It is important that you are concise and specific in your responses.

1. What is the single most important issue you would like help with now?

2. How is this affecting your life presently?

3. What would you like to achieve by the end of the <u>session</u> that would give you the sense that you had begun to make progress?

4. What have you done in the past that has helped even in a small way with the issue? Include your own attempts to help yourself and any therapy you have received on the issue.

5. What have you tried that has not helped with the issue? Again, please include your own attempts to help yourself and any therapy you have received on the issue.

6. Who in your life can support you as you tackle the issue now?

7. What strengths do you have as a person that may help you to address the issue?

8. Is there anything you think that it is vital for me to know in order to be able to help you with the issue?

Thank you.

Windy Dryden PhD

Table 19.2 Eugene's pre-session questionnaire

I invite you to fill in this questionnaire before your single session with me. It is a very important part of the process so please engage with the questions as much as you can. I have found that it helps people to prepare for their session with me so that they can get the most from it. It also helps me to help you as effectively as I can. Please return it by email attachment before our session. It is important that you are concise and specific in your responses.

1. What is the single most important issue you would like help with now?

> I have decided to apply for new jobs and there is a good chance that I will need to give a group presentation. I want to address my fear of giving such presentations, preferably before I have to give them.

2. How is this affecting your life presently?

> It's on my mind a lot and I am tempted not to apply for new jobs and play safe with my current job where I don't have to give presentations.

3. What would you like to achieve by the end of the <u>session</u> that would give you the sense that you had begun to make progress?

> I want to get some tips about how I can give presentations without being fearful.

4. What have you done in the past that has helped even in a small way with the issue? Include your own attempts to help yourself and any therapy you have received on the issue.

> Nothing has really helped apart from taking beta-blockers before group presentations at one point and alcohol at another point. I only did this when I could not get out of giving the presentation.

5. What have you tried that has not helped with the issue? Again, please include your own attempts to help yourself and any therapy you have received on the issue.

> I tried hypnosis but it was not helpful. The hypnotherapist recommended that I should imagine myself being very socially polished while giving a group presentation, but this did not help me deal with coming across as shy and awkward.

6. Who in your life can support you as you tackle the issue now?

I am not sure.

7. What strengths do you have as a person that may help you to address the issue?

Determination.

8. Is there anything you think that it is vital for me to know in order to be able to help you with the issue?

I can't think of anything.

Thank you.

Windy Dryden PhD

In the following ten chapters, I will discuss different facets of the session, starting with issues concerning beginning the session. But first, a word about making an appointment for the session. This session can be an intense experience for clients, and indeed there is a lot to get through, as you will see. For this reason, I recommend when making an appointment with a client for the session that you suggest that they nominate a time when they can give themself some time to focus their mind before the session and some time to reflect after the session. I suggest that they switch off their phone and other devices 30 minutes before the session to focus on what they want to achieve and refrain from switching these back on for at least 30 minutes after the session to give themself a chance to reflect on the session (see Chapter 29).

20

The session, 1: Beginning well

The model of SSI-CBT presented in this book is based on four stages. The session is the third stage. I will begin my discussion on the assumption that your client has completed and returned the pre-session questionnaire. In this and the following chapters, when I refer to the session, I mean the session where most of the work is done and which can take place face-to-face, online or over the telephone.

While there is no set way of beginning the session, here are several suggestions.

Update since the completion of the questionnaire

Since SSI-CBT is about facilitating movement, one way of implementing this is to ask the client at the beginning of the session to update their problem since they completed the pre-session questionnaire. I recommend doing this even if they completed the questionnaire very recently. If a change has occurred, then I suggest that you discover what the person did to effect such change. This information will help both of you see that the client may be able to effect change by doing more of what they did to improve. Suppose the person tried something new that did not effect change. In that case, it is vital that you discover what this was, distance yourself from it and use the ensuing discussion as a search for a new way of going forward for the client based on your input as an SSI-CBT therapist.

DOI: 10.4324/9781003214557-23

Beginning the session: Eugene

> *Windy:* Hello, Eugene. Nice to meet you. Perhaps I can start by asking you if you have noticed any changes in the problem since you completed the pre-session questionnaire?
>
> *Eugene:* Well, yes and no. I haven't given any group presentations, but I am keener to address the problem than before.
>
> *Windy:* What led to you feeling keener about addressing the problem?
>
> *Eugene:* Completing the questionnaire gave me a sense of hope that I could tackle the problem.

Beginning the session without the client's pre-session questionnaire

If the person has not completed a pre-session questionnaire for whatever reason, you can begin the session in a number of ways.

Ask a question about the purpose of the session

A good way of beginning an SSI-CBT session that assesses the client's knowledge of the service they have accessed involves asking the person a question about the purpose of the session.

> Q: From your perspective, what is the purpose of our conversation today?

If the person has an unrealistic expectation of the session's purpose, you will have an early opportunity to deal with this and point out what you can do and what you can't do in SSI-CBT.

Ask a question about the client's problem, concern or issue

It is most common that a client accesses SSI-CBT because they have a specific problem that they want to address. Given this, you can begin the session thus:

> Q: What problem, concern or issue would you like to discuss with me?
>
> Q: What problem, concern or issue would you like me to help you with?

Ask a question about the client's session goal

Instead of being problem-focused, an alternative is to begin the session by being goal-focused with particular reference to what the person wants to achieve from the session. Taking this stance, you could ask:

> Q: What would you like to achieve by talking with me today?
>
> Q: What would you like to take away from our conversation that would make it worthwhile that you came today?

Ask a question that focuses on help

Another way of beginning the SSI-CBT session is to focus on the concept of help. For example:

> Q: How can I be most helpful to you today?
>
> Q: What help would you like from me today?

These questions allow the client to specify the help that they want you to give them, what they want help with or both.

Once you have got the SSI-CBT process under way, your next task is to create a focus for the session, which is the subject of the next chapter.

The session, 2: Creating a focus

One of the essential skills you need to implement after initiating the SSI-CBT process is to help you and your client create a focus for the session. Obviously, time is limited in SSI-CBT; you have up to 50 minutes to complete the process, and therefore there is very little time for unfocused conversation. Having said that, some clients, as already noted, will want a more unfocused conversation as they wish to explore an issue or get things off their chest. However, in this chapter, I will discuss the situation where the client has nominated a problem with which they want help. Some of these clients may feel nervous at the outset and a bit of general talk, laced with some humour, helps put the client at ease. But once they are settled, the creation of a focus is paramount.

What is a focus?

Definitions of the word 'focus' emphasise the importance of centrality ('the centre of interest or activity') and clarity ('the state or quality of having or producing clear visual definition'). Thus, what you are looking for when you help your client to create a focus in SSI-CBT is a concentration on a clear, central point. Let me illustrate this using a vignette from one of my SSI-CBT 'cases'.

DOI: 10.4324/9781003214557-24

Windy: If we are to get the most out of this session, we need to focus on one clear issue or problem that you are looking for help with.

Client: Well, I get anxious in all sorts of situations.

(I can proceed in two ways here. First, I could ask the client to choose one such anxiety to focus on).

Windy: If you could choose one of these anxieties to concentrate on with me, an anxiety which, if I could help you with it, would make coming for single-session therapy well worth your while, what would it be?

(Second, I might ask the client if there is a prominent theme to these anxieties. This is the line I took in the session).

Windy: As you stand back and look at these anxieties, can you see a theme that links them?

Client: Well, I think they all involve me being judged by other people in some way.

Windy: Would it be a good idea for us to focus on your anxiety about being judged by other people throughout this session so I can help you deal with this eventuality in more constructive ways. Perhaps I could help you feel healthily concerned about being judged by others, rather than unhealthily anxious about it?

Client: Yes, that would be a good idea.

One important thing to note about this interchange is that the focus is on either *one* of the client's problems or the *one* theme that links the client's anxieties. In this book, I refer to this selected problem/theme as the nominated problem/issue.

The focus: problem, solution, goal or all three?

In solution-focused therapy (SFT), the focus is on the solution, not the problem, and if you integrate SFT into your work, you will help the person focus on the solution to their problem and not the problem itself. SSI-CBT can accommodate this stance. My position is more in line with traditional CBT, and the focus I strive to create includes the person's problem, their goal with respect to the problem, and the solution to the problem. This is precisely what I did in the 'case vignette' above where I said, 'Would it be a good idea for us to focus on your anxiety about being judged by other people [the client's problem] throughout this session so I can help you deal with this eventuality in more constructive ways [solution]. Perhaps, I could help you feel healthily concerned about being judged by others, rather than unhealthily anxious about it?' [my suggestion for a goal for the client]

At this stage of the SSI-CBT process, it is not so important to be very specific about the person's problem, as you will want to define this more specifically soon. Having said this, if you are presented with an opportunity to define the problem specifically at the same time as you are creating a focus, then take it, as doing so will save a little time – and, as you should know by now, time is at a premium in SSI-CBT. The important issue about creating a focus with respect to the solution is that you cover it, and it is OK to be vague about it at this stage. This is precisely what I did when I said to the client, '…so I can help you deal with this eventuality in more constructive ways'. Thus, a focus should include the fact that you will be helping the client to find a solution to their problem and not so much what that solution will be. You will do this when you define the client's problem precisely. This will help you set a specific goal concerning this defined problem and find a specific solution that effectively addresses the person's problem and helps them move towards their problem-related goal. Parenthetically, the client's session goal is frequently a vague reference to wanting to find a solution. My language 'deal with this eventuality in more constructive ways' points to a vague solution which we will make more concrete later in the session.

Finally, let me clarify that creating a focus that just incorporates the client's problem without a corresponding goal or solution is neither good practice in ongoing CBT nor SSI-CBT, as it gives you both nothing for which to aim. Thus, avoid doing so, if at all possible.

Keeping to the focus or changing it

Once you have created a focus, you need to help the person keep to that focus unless there is a good reason to change it. The two main good reasons to change a focus in the session once you have created it are as follows. First, it becomes clear that the initially created focus was inaccurate. You may have made what I call a 'false start' in SSI-CBT and need to make a better start by creating a more accurate focus. Second, keeping to the original focus may threaten the working alliance between you and your client, and thus you need to change focus to preserve this alliance. Of course, changing an already created focus means that you have not used time as productively as you could have, but keeping to an inaccurate focus is both wasteful of your remaining time and poor therapeutic practice.

Prepare the client for possible interruption and interrupt with tact

Some clients find it relatively easy to focus once the focus has been jointly created and only need to be gently nudged back to that focus when they stray from it. Others need more than a gentle nudge to do so. They need to be interrupted. There are two main issues to be considered about interrupting a client who has strayed from the focus and cannot be nudged back to that focus. First, it is best to prepare all clients for the possibility of interrupting them and, in doing so, it is good to provide them with a rationale for such interruption and seek their permission to do so. Here is an example of what I say in this respect:

> *Windy:* There may be times when I need to interrupt you. The purpose of me doing this is to help you keep to the focus we have agreed and sometimes, being human, you may stray a bit too far from that focus which means that we lose valuable time. So, if this happens, can I have your permission to interrupt you?

My experience is that when you give a rationale for interrupting a client, and they give permission for you to do so, then interrupting them causes minimum disruption. Indeed, some clients will actively want you to interrupt them since they acknowledge that they tend to go off track and welcome being brought back to the agreed focus.

The second issue to be considered is your attitude and comfort level concerning interrupting a client. Some people new to SSI-CBT are reluctant to interrupt clients because they think it is anti-therapeutic or rude. Concerning the first issue, I would argue that it is anti-therapeutic *not* to interrupt a client in SSI-CBT since the time that you spend letting them talk away from the focus will, generally, not lead to good results. Indeed, it will prevent you from helping the client achieve what they came for from SSI-CBT. On the second point, as long as you do so with tact, having explained the purpose of the interruption and sought permission to do so, it is hardly rude to interrupt your client. Rudeness in this respect is when you interrupt a client (1) without tact, (2) without presenting a rationale and (3) without having sought and been given permission to do so.

Finally, if you are uncomfortable about interrupting clients, I suggest that you interrupt them while feeling uncomfortable until you can do so without discomfort. Doing role-plays with colleagues where they play a client who can't be nudged back to a focus and you interrupt them will help in this respect.

Creating the focus: Eugene

Windy:	So, based on the pre-session questionnaire you completed, what problem do we need to focus on in the session?
Eugene:	My anxiety about giving group presentations and my attitude towards giving them.
Windy:	And what do you want to achieve from the session?
Eugene:	I want to change my attitude so I can give group presentations rather than avoid them as I am currently doing.

There are two points to make about this exchange. First, it is a little unusual for a client to feature their attitude and attitude change in creating a therapeutic focus. Encouraging, but unusual. I see this 'attitude' as forming the solution to Eugene's problem and, as such, it will help him achieve his goal of giving rather than avoiding group presentations. Second, the problem and goal have been loosely described, which is acceptable for creating the focus in SSI-CBT. A more comprehensive understanding of both will be achieved later in the session.

In this chapter, I have discussed the important issue of helping the client create a focus for the session and keeping to this focus once it has been created. In the next chapter, I will discuss how to help the client understand their problem more thoroughly.

22

The session, 3: Understanding the nominated problem

After you have helped your client create a focus, the next step is to help them do two things. First, enable the person to state their nominated problem (i.e. the one problem that they selected to address in SSI-CBT) so that you can both understand it more clearly (which will be the focus of this chapter) and, second, help the person to set a goal in relation to this nominated problem (which is the subject of Chapter 23). If they have not yet had a chance to do so, allow your client to express their nominated problem in their own words. When they do so, I suggest listening to what they say using whatever assessment framework you employ and using it when clarifying what they are saying. This is likely to be some version of the 'ABC' framework that is commonly employed in CBT.

Problem understanding includes relevant information about the problem placed at 'A' and 'C'. As we will see in the following chapter, goal setting consists of the same data at 'A' that appears in the problem and more constructive responses at 'C'.

Understanding the nominated problem

As I said above, understanding the problem involves finding out information concerning the person's responses at 'C' to the adversity they actually faced or thought they faced at 'A'. Usually, in CBT, information about 'A' and 'C' is collected before the person is helped to see that their 'B' (problematic cognitions) are at the root of the problematic responses at 'C' to the adversity at 'A'. For this reason, I have left the topic of the assessment of 'B' until Chapter 24.

Understanding responses at 'C'

The primary response systems you will want to understand concerning your client's nominated problem are emotional, physiological, behavioural and cognitive.

Emotional responses at 'C'

In my experience, clients tend to bring eight problematic negative emotions to SSI-CBT. The ones that they readily nominate for change are anxiety, depression, guilt and jealousy. They tend to be ambivalent about changing anger, while shame, hurt and envy tend to be a feature of some of their problems, but they need to be helped to see this.

Physiological responses at 'C'

Different people respond differently physiologically at 'C' to adversities at 'A', with perhaps the most significant variability in physiological responsiveness occurring in anxiety. While people react physiologically to adversities, they can then focus on their reaction, which then becomes an 'A', about which they may further disturb themselves. This phenomenon is known as a meta-problem, and I will discuss it further later in this chapter.

Behavioural responses at 'C'

In my view, you need to be interested in two types of behavioural responses. The first type involves behaviours that are associated with the emotional responses listed above. For example, when your client experiences anxiety, they will tend to withdraw from the threat. When I train people in SSI-CBT (WD), I suggest that they learn the main ways people tend to act when they experience each of the problematic emotions listed above (see Dryden, 2022b). Whatever approach to CBT you practise, you may benefit from learning this material.

The second type of behavioural responses that you need to be interested in involves behaviours that people engage in that protect them from the adversity. These include avoidance behaviours, safety-seeking behaviours, reassurance-seeking behaviours, overcompensatory behaviours, the use of alcohol and drugs, and facing less aversive situations.

You need to discover which specific behaviours in their nominated problem the person enacts in both types of behavioural response discussed above.

Cognitive responses at 'C'

The 'ABC' framework indicates that people disturb themselves at 'C' about the adversities in their life at 'A' because of their views of these adversities at 'B'. So far, we have considered the emotional, physiological and behavioural components of disturbance. The final component that I want to discuss involves cognitive responses to adversity. These include the inferences people make when disturbed, which tend to be heavily skewed to the negative, the ruminations that people engage in when they are disturbed, and how they process information when they are disturbed. In addition, you need to understand the cognitions that people engage in when they seek to protect themselves from the adversity. These are the cognitive equivalents to avoidance, safety seeking, reassurance seeking and overcompensatory behaviours.

It is important to remember that you don't have time to be comprehensive in the data you collect about your client's 'C' concerning their nominated problem. However, it would help if you had the breadth of knowledge to discover their problem's major 'C' factors.

Understanding the adversity at 'A'

Once you have understood the significant components of your client's disturbed response to the adversity in their nominated problem, you need to understand the nature of this adversity. There are two primary components of the adversity. The first is the situation in which the problem occurred, and the second is the aspect of the situation about which the person was most disturbed. This is likely to be inferential in nature. This latter component is usually the most important to understand.

Situational 'A'

I call the situation in which the adversity occurs the situational 'A'. It is usually reflected in more descriptive accounts of the problem. Thus, when Eugene says that he is anxious about giving group presentations, 'giving group presentations' is the situational 'A'.

Inferential 'A'

In Chapter 5, I made the point that, if possible, it is important that you help your client deal healthily with their adversity, and I mentioned above that this is likely to be inferential in nature. Also in Chapter 5, I listed the main inferences associated with each of the eight problematic emotions for which people tend to seek help. In training people in SSI-CBT (WD), I suggest that they learn these inference–emotion associations to search out the inferential adversity when working with the primary disturbed emotion involved in the nominated problem. Whichever approach to CBT you practise, it is vital that you become versed in the type of 'As' that go along with each of the 'Cs' that your clients are likely to bring to SSI-CBT.

Identifying the adversity: the 'magic question' technique. There are many ways of assessing the inferential 'A' in SSI-CBT. However, one of my favourite methods is the 'magic question' technique (Dryden, 2022a). Here is how to use this technique:

- Step 1: Have the client focus on their disturbed emotional 'C' (e.g. 'anxiety')
- Step 2: Have the client focus on the situation in which 'C' occurred (e.g. 'about to give a public presentation to a group of consultants')
- Step 3: Ask the client: *'Which ingredient could we give you to eliminate or significantly reduce "C" (here, anxiety)?'* (In this case, the client said: 'My mind not going blank.') Take care that the client does not change the situation (i.e. they do not say: 'Not giving the presentation')
- Step 4: The opposite is probably 'A' (e.g. 'My mind going blank'), but check. Ask: *'So when you were about to give the presentation, were you most anxious about your mind going blank?'* If not, use the question again until the client confirms what they were most anxious about in the described situation

Looking for the presence of a meta-problem and deciding whether to make this the nominated problem

In Chapter 4, I discussed the concept of the meta-problem.[1] This describes the uniquely human phenomenon whereby having disturbed themself about an adversity at 'A', the person then focuses on their response, an aspect of which becomes another adversity for the person who then disturbs themself about this second problem. In ongoing therapy, you would deal with the meta-problem before the original problem only if its presence prevented the original problem from being tackled both inside and outside therapy and if the client could see the sense of doing so. In SSI-CBT, where time is at a premium, it should only be tackled, in my view, if it is, in fact, the client's main problem. Suppose they realise that it is, then fine, but if not you need to provide the client with a rationale for your viewpoint and why it should be the focus of the work and become the client's nominated problem. An example of this is where the client experiences a lot of shame about their problems. However, if the client is clear that they want to focus on their original nominated problem and not their meta-problem, you should respect this.

Understanding the nominated problem: Eugene

Windy:	So, let me find out a little more about your anxiety about giving group presentations. Do you have a group presentation coming up, or could you arrange one?
Eugene:	Yes, I could.
Windy:	Imagine that you are about to give the presentation. Which aspect of giving such a presentation are you most anxious about?

(In the 'ABC' framework that I use, 'A' stands for adversity. This includes the situations that people have problems about (in Eugene's case, the group presentations) and what it is about these situations that they find aversive. I am now going to try and find out what this adversity is. Note that I am working with a specific future example of the client's problem here. As I explained earlier, I am doing so because this will help the client more easily put into practice whatever they may learn from the SSI-CBT process the next time they encounter the situation in which they are likely to experience their problem).

Eugene:	Well, I may get nervous, and people may see this.
Windy:	Which of those do you get most anxious about… getting nervous or people seeing you get nervous?
Eugene:	Both the same.

Windy:	Let's take these things one at a time. What anxious meaning are you giving to getting nervous?
Eugene:	I think it means that I have a defect.
Windy:	And what anxious meaning are you giving to people seeing you get nervous?
Eugene:	That they also think that I have a defect.

(So, Eugene's 'A' is 'Giving a group presentation and showing myself and others that I have a defect by getting nervous and being seen to get nervous').

Windy:	What do you do when you are anxious in this situation?
Eugene:	Well, I try to get out of giving them if I can.
Windy:	So, you avoid them. What if you can't avoid them?
Eugene:	Well, I either do a lot of preparation and practice. Too much.
Windy:	So, you over-prepare and over-rehearse?
Eugene:	Yes.
Windy:	Anything else?
Eugene:	Well, just before I give a presentation, I have a few shots of whisky to calm my nerves.
Windy:	What about in the room? How do you try to hide your symptoms?
Eugene:	I give a PowerPoint and turn my back on the group and talk to the screen.
Windy:	Now, when your anxiety has kicked in, what thoughts do you have?
Eugene:	I think that people are waiting for me to screw up.

Here is a summary of Eugene's problem using the 'ABC' framework that I employ. You will note that I have divided the 'A' into its situational and inferential components.

'A' (Situational): Giving a group presentation
'A' (Inferential): I will be nervous, which means that I have
        a defect. The group will see that I am nervous and think
        I have a defect

'B' (Problematic Cognitions): Not assessed yet

'C' (Emotion): Anxiety
'C' (Behavioural): Avoidance (of 'A')
        If can't avoid 'A': • Over-prepare and over-rehearse in
                                advance
                            • Take alcohol before going into
                                the room
                            • Hide from the group in the room
'C' (Cognitive): People are waiting for me to screw up

Generalising from the nominated problem

I mentioned earlier in this book that one of the skills that the SSI-CBT therapist needs to develop is to move, with ease, from a specific focus to a general focus and back again, if necessary. In this chapter, I have discussed how to identify your client's nominated problem. Now would be a good time to enquire whether the problem is experienced in contexts other than the one that frames the nominated problem. Here is how I did this with Eugene.

Windy: So, the main thing that you are anxious about with respect to giving a group presentation is that you will reveal to yourself and others that you have a defect if you get nervous. Is that right?

Eugene: That's right.

Windy: Is this a problem for you in other situations?

Eugene: Yes. It occurs basically in any situation where the focus is on me and where I may show some weakness.

Windy: And you get anxious about such situations?

Eugene: Yes, I try to avoid them if I possibly can.

Windy: So, although our main focus will be on you giving group presentations, is it worth considering how you might generalise what you learn about handling these presentations to other situations where the focus is on you and where you may reveal a defect or weakness to yourself and others?

Eugene: That would be great if we could do that.

While I covered the issue of generalisation before helping Eugene find a solution to his problem, this topic can also be addressed after the solution has been selected, rehearsed and a plan to implement it developed.

Having considered understanding the nominated problem in this chapter, in the next chapter I will discuss setting goals in general in SSI-CBT and with respect to the nominated problem, in particular.

Note

1   Meta-problem here means the problem about the problem.

23

The session, 4: Setting a goal

Session goals and problem-related goals

After you have helped yourself and your client to understand the 'A' and 'C' features of their nominated problem, you are in a good position to ask your client about their goals. In SSI-CBT, there are two different goals: *session goals*, or what the client wants to achieve from the session they are having with you, and *problem-related goals*, or what they want to achieve related to their nominated problem.

Session goal questions

When you ask a client about a session goal, the language in your question needs to reflect this. Here are some good examples of session goal questions.

- 'What would you take away from the session that would make it worthwhile that you came today?'
- 'What would you take away from the session that would give you a sense that you could effectively deal with the issue you came with?'
- 'What would you take away from the session that would help you get unstuck?'

DOI: 10.4324/9781003214557-26

In my experience, when a person responds to questions about a session goal, their answers are often vague, but I see them as embryonic forms of a more specific solution to their nominated problem. For example:

- 'I'm looking for some tips to help me with my anxiety'
- 'I'm hoping that you might give me some tools to help me to deal with my problem'
- 'It would good if you could help me to look at things differently'

Problem-related goals

As I mentioned earlier, a problem-related goal is a goal that relates to the person's problem. Please note that if you ask your client for a problem-related goal after you and your client have arrived at an assessment of the problem, then your question will be informed by that assessment. Therefore, you will likely get a more valuable and clear goal in this circumstance than if you asked the same question before problem assessment.

For example, if your client is coming to SSI-CBT for help with public speaking anxiety before you have assessed the problem, you might ask the client:

- 'How would you like to feel about giving a public speech?' [Question not informed by problem assessment]

After the assessment, you might ask them:

- 'Instead of responding to your mind going blank with anxiety (the client's problematic response), what would an acceptable constructive response be to this happening?' [Question informed by problem assessment]

The importance of setting a goal in response to the adversity (inferential 'A') rather than in response to the situational 'A'

Often when people discuss their problems in therapy, they talk about their disturbed responses to the actual situations that they find problematic. As discussed earlier, I call these situations 'situational As'. Thus, when Eugene first told me what he wanted to focus on in SSI-CBT, he said he was anxious about giving group presentations. When we looked further, we found out what it was about giving group presentations that made Eugene most anxious: revealing a defect to himself and others by getting nervous. In the 'ABC' framework that I use, giving group presentations is Eugene's situational 'A' and revealing a defect to self and others is his inferential 'A'. My view is that Eugene's inferential 'A' is his adversity.

Suppose people tend to identify situational 'As' when they nominate their problem. In that case, they do the same when discussing their goal unless guided to set a goal concerning their adversity (usually their inferential 'A'). You will probably have to give them a rationale for providing such guidance, which they need to accept before you both proceed. I deal with this issue with Eugene, as can be seen at the end of the chapter.

Helping your client to construct healthy responses to the adversity

Once your client understands the importance of setting a goal concerning facing their adversity, your next task is to help them construct healthy responses to that adversity. This will serve as their goal for their nominated problem.

In my view, the best way to do this is to take the 'AC' components that you identified when working to understand the problem. The 'A' components were the situation in which the problem occurred (the situational 'A') and what the person was most disturbed about (the inferential 'A'). As I have said, in my view, the inferential 'A' is most often the adversity. When setting a goal with the client, keep these 'A' components the same. Otherwise, the person will not be helped to deal with their adversity constructively. The 'C' components are the emotional, behavioural and cognitive responses to the adversity. In helping the person construct healthy responses, ideally you need to help them identify alternative healthy responses to each unhealthy response in the three response categories listed above, i.e. emotional, behavioural and cognitive. I have provided an example of this at the end of the chapter from my work with Eugene.

Healthy behavioural responses

Perhaps the most straightforward healthy responses to construct are behavioural. As I will discuss below, it is important, if possible, to help the person nominate the presence of a healthy behaviour rather than the absence of an unhealthy behaviour.

Healthy cognitive responses

When constructing healthy cognitive responses to the adversity, i.e. responses that accompany emotions at 'C' rather than those that mediate (at 'B') responses to the adversity at 'A', a useful rule of thumb is as follows. Healthy cognitive responses are balanced and incorporate negative, neutral and positive features of 'A' (e.g. 'Some people may judge me negatively for showing my nervousness, some will be compassionate towards me, and some won't even notice'). In contrast, unhealthy cognitive responses are highly distorted and skewed to the negative (e.g. 'Everyone will judge me negatively for showing my nervousness').

Healthy emotional responses

As I discussed in Chapter 5, when your client comes to SSI-CBT struggling in the face of an adversity, SSI-CBT provides them with an opportunity to deal constructively with that adversity. In some forms of CBT, the emphasis is on helping clients see that their inferential 'A's are distorted and the thrust will be on helping them by questioning these distorted inferences. While this stance is often helpful, it does not assist your client in dealing constructively with adversity from their frame of reference. In addition, it is not inconceivable that they may encounter situations where their inferences turn out to be correct. Thus, while Eugene may distort reality by assuming that people will think he has a defect if he reveals being nervous while giving a group presentation, this may, in fact, happen. As such, my approach is founded on the idea that he needs to be helped to deal with this eventuality.[1]

When a person has a problem with an adversity, they usually experience a negative emotion. I call this negative emotion unhealthy when it leads the person to get stuck. It is associated with various unconstructive behavioural and cognitive responses and discourages the person from facing and dealing constructively with the adversity. On the other hand, when the person responds constructively to the adversity, they also experience a negative emotion. Why? Because the adversity is negative, and it is healthy to feel negative when something negative happens. I call this negative emotion healthy when it leads the person to get unstuck. It is associated with various constructive behavioural and cognitive responses and encourages the person to face and deal constructively with the adversity.

Negotiating a healthy emotional response to an adversity can often be quite tricky with a client since people generally think that such a response involves the diminution or absence of an unhealthy negative emotion rather than the presence of a healthy negative one. Also, in the English language, we do not have terms that denote healthy negative emotions in a way that clearly differentiates them from unhealthy negative emotions. Consequently, it is important that you negotiate with your client terms for both the unhealthy negative emotion that they experience in their nominated problem and the healthy negative emotion which they will experience if they reach their goal.

Dealing with obstacles to effective goal-setting in SSI-CBT

Even though time is at a premium in SSI-CBT (an oft-repeated refrain in this book!), it is worth taking your time to help your client set a realistic goal. In particular, there are several obstacles to deal with while effectively setting such a goal. Here are some of the most common barriers and brief guidelines concerning how to respond if you encounter them in SSI-CBT.

When your client sets a vague goal

Your client may set a vague goal. If so, it is important that you help them make this goal as specific as possible for their desired emotional, behavioural and, if relevant, cognitive responses to the adversity at 'A'.

When your client wants to change 'A'

Often your client may wish to change 'A', either the situational 'A' or the inferential 'A', rather than changing their unconstructive responses to the 'A' to constructive ones. If this is the case and 'A' can be changed, help them to understand that the best chance they have to change 'A' is when they are in a healthy frame of mind to do so, and this is achieved when their responses to this 'A' are constructive. So, before they can change 'A', they need to change their 'C'.

When your client wants to change another person

When your client's nominated problem is centred on their relationship to another person or group of people, their goal may be to change the other(s). You need to help your client see that this goal is inappropriate as others' behaviour is not under the direct control of your client. However, attempts to influence others are under your client's direct control and *may* lead to behavioural change. As such, they are appropriate goals. However, it is often important to help the client consider their responses if their influence attempts do not work in these cases. Assisting clients to deal constructively with such failed attempts is often vital in such cases.

When your client sets a goal based on experiencing less of the problematic response

When asked about their goals concerning the adversity at 'A', clients often say that they want to feel less of the disturbed emotion featured in their nominated problem (e.g. less anxious). Many CBT therapists may accept this as a legitimate goal, but it is problematic in SSI-CBT (WD) for the following reason. REBT theory, which underpins SSI-CBT (WD), argues that when a client holds a rigid attitude, they take a preference (e.g. for acceptance) and make it rigid (e.g. 'I want to be accepted, and therefore I have to be'). When they hold a flexible attitude, they take the same preference and keep it flexible by negating possible rigidity (e.g. 'I want to be accepted, but I don't need to be'). In both the rigid attitude and the flexible attitude, the strength of the unhealthy negative emotion in the first case and the healthy negative emotion in the second is determined by the strength of the preference when that preference is not met. The stronger the preference under these circumstances, the stronger the negative emotion of both types. Thus, in SSI-CBT (WD), my goal is to help the person experience a healthy negative emotion of relative intensity to the unhealthy negative emotion rather than to encourage them to strive to experience an unhealthy negative emotion of decreased intensity.

When your client sets a goal based on experiencing the absence of the problematic response

You also need to be prepared when your client nominates the absence of the problem as their goal (e.g. 'I don't want to feel anxious when giving a talk'). When your client says this, it is important to help them see that it is not possible to live in a response vacuum, and from there you can discuss the presence of a set of healthy responses to their adversity as their goal.

When your client sets as a goal a positive response to the situational 'A' and bypasses the adversity

Another situation that may well occur when you ask a client for their goal is that they nominate a positive response to the situational 'A' while bypassing the adversity (usually the inferential 'A'). For example, if Eugene had taken this tack, he would have said something like: 'I want to become confident at giving group presentations.' However, in doing so, he would have bypassed his dealing with the adversity, which was revealing a defect to self and others by getting nervous. Thus, a good response to Eugene would be to ask him how he could become confident at giving group presentations as long as he regarded becoming nervous as revealing a defect to himself and others. By helping Eugene deal with this first and setting an appropriate goal concerning his adversity, you will help him take the next step and increase his confidence about his performance. Taking this approach is akin to a situation where you want to get to Windsor from London by train, but the only way of doing so is to go to Slough and change trains there to Windsor, as there is no direct train from London to Windsor.

Setting a goal concerning the nominated problem: Eugene

Windy: Now that we are clear about what you are anxious about and what some of the main features of your anxiety are, let's discuss what you want to achieve from this session. OK?

Eugene:	OK.
Windy:	What would you like to achieve by discussing this?
Eugene:	I would like to be able to handle giving group presentations better.

(Note that when I ask an open-ended question about goals, Eugene gives a general answer about dealing with his situational 'A' rather than his inferential 'A'. I now help him focus on his adversity (i.e. his inferential 'A') before helping him set a goal with respect to his adversity).

Windy:	Do you think that you will be able to do this if we first deal with the issue of what you call your defects or if we don't deal with them?
Eugene:	If we deal with them.
Windy:	OK, let me first summarise. We have discovered that what you are most anxious about concerning giving group presentations is your inference that getting nervous indicates that you have a defect and that if others see you get anxious, they will also think that you have a defect. Correct?
Eugene:	Yes.
Windy:	As we have seen, being anxious about such adversities is not helping you, so what would be a more constructive response to having a defect and being seen by others to have the defect, assuming for the moment that it is a defect and others will share this view?

(In other CBT approaches, the therapeutic emphasis may well be on helping Eugene to re-evaluate the inferential meaning that he places on getting nervous – i.e. it is a defect – and the inferential prediction about others' response

to his nervousness, i.e. they will regard his nervousness as a defect. In SSI-CBT (WD), the initial focus is on assuming that inferences are valid temporarily to identify and explore evaluative meaning. This is more consistent with REBT, the primary CBT approach that informs SSI-CBT (WD).)

Eugene: To not be concerned about it.

(As I indicated above, people often nominate a lack of emotional response as a therapeutic goal, and I discussed the importance of not accepting this as a legitimate goal for SSI-CBT.)

Windy: The only way I can help you do that is to have you lie to yourself and believe that it doesn't matter if you have, or are seen by others to have, a defect. Is that possible?

Eugene: No, I guess not.

Windy: So how about if I help you to have an alternative negative emotion about the prospect of revealing a defect, an emotion whereby you don't feel you have to drink alcohol beforehand but can have water, and where you can face the audience during the presentation rather than hide from them? And an emotion that will lead you to think that most people aren't waiting for you to screw up, even if some might be. How would that suit you?

(What I have done here is the following: (1) I have indicated that it is healthy to experience a negative emotion ('C') in the face of an adversity ('A') and thus provided a realistic alternative to not feeling concerned; (2) I have put forward the constructive behavioural alternatives to the client's unconstructive behaviours; and (3) I have put forward a more balanced cognitive response that accompanies concern

as opposed to the highly negatively skewed cognition that accompanied Eugene's anxiety).

Eugene:	Well, that sounds more realistic, so yes.
Windy:	OK, I would call this emotion concern without anxiety. Does that make sense?
Eugene:	Yes, so you distinguish between anxious and concern without anxiety?
Windy:	Yes, I do.
Eugene:	OK.

Here is a summary of Eugene's goal using the 'ABC' framework that I employ. You will notice that both the situational and inferential components of 'A' are the same in Eugene's problem as in his goal. This reflects my preferred practice of helping people deal constructively with adversity, whether real or imagined, before they try to change the adversity (if it is real and can be changed) or question 'A' (if it is distorted).

'A' (Situational): Giving a group presentation

'A' (Inferential): I will be nervous, which means that I have a defect. The group will see that I am nervous and think I have a defect

'B' (Healthy Cognitions): Not assessed yet

'C' (Emotion): Concern, but not anxious

'C' (Behavioural): Face 'A'

- Prepare and rehearse for the presentation without over-preparing and over-rehearsing.
- Drink water rather than alcohol before going into the room
- Face the group in the room rather than hide from them

'C' (Cognitive): Some people may be waiting for me to screw up, but most won't be

Generalising from the goal

At the end of the last chapter, I mentioned that it is important for the SSI-CBT therapist to move freely from a specific focus to a general focus and back again. In this context, once you and your client have understood the latter's nominated problem and its 'A' and 'C' components, it is important for you to check with your client whether they experience the same problem in other contexts. If so, it is important to help your client see that they can generalise any learning they derive from SSI-CBT regarding their nominated problem to these other situations and that you will help them do this, if required. If the client has indicated that their nominated problem is an example of a more general problem, then the same issue can be raised concerning their goals. Therefore, you can ask if the goal they have selected concerning their nominated problem is also what they would like to aim for more broadly whenever they experience their more general problem.

Here is how I did this with Eugene:

Windy:	So earlier we ascertained that your anxiety about giving a group presentation is a specific example of a more general problem about revealing a weakness when the focus of social attention is on you. The goal we have set for this problem when it occurs in a group presentation context is for you to feel concerned but not anxious about revealing a defect to yourself and others, but to face the situation and to face the other people in the situation without finding ways to hide from them, and to do all this without using alcohol. Also, to prepare and rehearse for the presentation without over-preparing and over-rehearsing for it. Is that correct?
Eugene:	Yes, it is.
Windy:	Now, would that goal also hold when you think of facing other situations when the focus is on

> | | you, and you may reveal a defect to yourself and others? |
> |---|---|
> | *Eugene:* | Yes, in general it would be. |
> | *Windy:* | So, while we keep our focus on handling giving group presentations more constructively, shall we look for ways in which you could also achieve the same goals in these other relevant anxiety-provoking contexts? |
> | *Eugene:* | That would be great. |

In this chapter, I dealt with session goals and problem-related goals. Concerning the latter, I discussed how you could help your client understand the 'A' and 'C' components of their nominated problem and set a suitable goal at 'C' with respect to the same 'A'. In the next chapter, I will consider the topic of helping your client to understand the problematic cognitions at 'B' that mediate between 'A' and 'C'.

Note

1   Assuming, of course, that Eugene sees the sense of doing so.

24

The session, 5: Identifying the central mechanism

Introduction

Epictetus's famous dictum, 'People are disturbed not by things, but by the views they take of them', has been put forward as a saying that describes, in a nutshell, the role of cognition in the emotional disorders. In the 'ABC' framework that most CBT therapists use, 'B' describes the cognitions that we hold about the adversity at 'A' that explain our responses to that adversity at 'C'. As I explained in Chapter 4, different approaches to CBT have different views about the nature and importance of 'B' in accounting for and the treatment of psychological disturbance. In CBT approaches that hold the view that problematic cognitions or meanings explain such disturbances and need to be modified, such cognitions are variously described according to the approach. Here is a partial list of these problematic cognitions:

- Negative automatic thoughts
- Cognitive distortions
- Dysfunctional assumptions
- Irrational beliefs
- Maladaptive schemas

In addition to these verbal constructs, there are images to be taken into consideration as well.

These problematic cognitions are what I refer to in the book as the 'central mechanism' as they tend to account for the problematic responses that the person has made to the adversity in question.

DOI: 10.4324/9781003214557-27

Suppose you are a CBT therapist who believes that it is vital to identify and deal with problematic cognitions by helping clients to modify them. In that case, you will look for those cognitions which your approach tends to prioritise, and you will help your clients examine and change them using a variety of methods that need to be employed in ways framed by the time restrictions of SSI-CBT.

Suppose you are a CBT therapist who believes that your client's engagement with these so-called problematic cognitions rather than the presence of such cognitions themselves is the problem (i.e. the central mechanism). In that case, you will find ways to encourage them to accept these cognitions mindfully rather than engage with them or try to eliminate them and thence to commit themselves to value-based action.

In this chapter, I will consider identifying the central mechanism, usually in the form of problematic cognitions. In the next chapter, I will look at how to deal with them and help the person develop a more constructive central mechanism. The best way to discuss the role of identifying and dealing with central mechanisms in SSI-CBT is to show how I approach these two issues in SSI-CBT (WD). While I do employ mindfulness and acceptance-based techniques in my work, my approach to the two issues is firmly in the modification-based camp.

Identifying the central mechanism (problematic cognitions) in SSI-CBT (WD)

So far in the practice part of this book, I have discussed creating a focus and working with a nominated problem by understanding the adversity at the heart of the problem (at 'A' in the 'ABC' framework) and the person's responses to this adversity at 'C' and setting a goal concerning this nominated problem.

The next step is to help my client understand the role that cognitions play in (1) their nominated problem and (2) their goal concerning that problem. I will help the client identify specifically what these cognitions are in the first case and what healthier cognitions might be developed in the second case. I do this in the following way:

1. I review with my client what we know and what we don't know as a result of identifying the 'A' and 'C' components of the nominated problem and their goal, respectively.

Windy:	So let's review what we know and what we don't know. We know that when you have to give a group presentation, you feel anxious about doing so. We also know that what you are most anxious about in this situation is getting nervous, revealing to you and your audience that you have a defect. Is that correct?
Eugene:	Yes, that's right.
Windy:	We also know that you would much prefer not to have such a defect and reveal it to others. Is that right?
Eugene:	Yes.

(*What I am doing here is making explicit the first stage of my assessment of Eugene's attitudes. In REBT theory, a rigid attitude and a flexible attitude have a common core: in Eugene's case, his preference not to have a defect and for others not to see it. Please note that I have not yet challenged his inferences that (1) getting nervous is a defect and (2) others present will also see it as a defect. If I need to do this, it will be after I have helped Eugene to develop a flexible attitude towards these adversities*).

Windy:	What we don't know yet is what your anxiety is based on and what your emotional goal towards this adversity could be based on. So please help me out here. OK?
Eugene:	OK.

2. I then take the client's preference (which is common to both rigid and flexible attitudes) and ask the client whether their nominated problem is based on their rigid attitude or their flexible attitude.

> *Windy:* So when you are anxious about giving a group presentation, is your anxiety based on attitude 1, that you prefer not to have such a defect and for others not to see it and therefore both these things must not happen, or on attitude 2, that you prefer not to have such a defect and for others not to see it, but unfortunately that does not mean that both of these things must not happen?
>
> *Eugene:* When I am anxious, my anxiety is based on the first attitude you outlined.
>
> (*What I have done here is to help Eugene see that a problematic cognition is at the core of his problem and that this is expressed in the form of a rigid attitude. Please note that here I am guided by REBT theory. Other CBT therapists will be guided by whatever theory underpins their approach to CBT*).

3. I then ask the client how they would feel if they had a firm conviction in the alternative flexible attitude and connect this attitude with their goal.

> *Windy:* And how would you feel if you had a firm conviction in the other attitude, that you prefer not to have such a defect and for others not to see it, but unfortunately that does not mean that both of these things must not happen?

Eugene:	Well, if I really believed it, I would feel what you called concern.
Windy:	Which is what we agreed was the emotional goal we would aim for.
Eugene:	That's right.
Windy:	So, can you see that when you take your preference not to have the defect of getting nervous in group presentations and for others not to see this defect, and you make this preference rigid, you create feelings of anxiety?
Eugene:	Yes, I can see that.
Windy:	And can you see that when you keep the preference flexible, you are concerned but not anxious about giving group presentations and the prospect of getting nervous and others present seeing this and thinking as you do that you have a defect?
Eugene:	Yes, I can.
Windy:	What do I need to help you do to work towards your goal?
Eugene:	To help me to believe in the flexible attitude.

In Table 24.1, I present a summary of Eugene's 'ABC' assessment for both his nominated problem and for his goal in relation to his problem. Note again that his 'A' is the same in both.

4. At the end of a piece of work in identifying the central mechanism in the form of problematic cognitions (rigid attitude) in my client's nominated problem and the new central mechanism in the form of healthy alternative cognitions (flexible attitude) in their goal, I do the following. First, I enquire if these two sets of cognitions are also present in other contexts in which the client's problem occurs and their goal is relevant. If I have

been accurate in my cognitive assessment, these two sets of cognitions are generally present. In which case, I encourage my client to look for these when dealing with the problem in these other contexts.

Table 24.1 Eugene's 'ABC' assessment for his nominated problem and his problem-related goal

Nominated problem	Goal
'A' (Situational): Giving a group presentation	**'A' (Situational):** Giving a group presentation
'A' (Inferential):	**'A' (Inferential):**
(1) I will be nervous which means that I have a defect	(1) I will be nervous which means that I have a defect
(2) The group will see that I am nervous and think I have a defect	(2) The group will see that I am nervous and think I have a defect
'B' (Rigid attitude): 'I prefer not to have such a defect of getting nervous and I prefer that others don't see it and therefore both these things must not happen'	**'B' (Flexible attitude):** 'I prefer not to have such a defect and I prefer that others don't see it, but unfortunately that does not mean that both of these things must not happen'
'C' (Behavioural 1): Avoidance **(Behavioural 2):** If I can't avoid 'A': • Over-prepare and over-rehearse in advance • Take alcohol before going into the room • Hide from the group in the room	**'C' (Behavioural):** Face 'A': • Prepare and rehearse for the presentation without over-preparation and over-rehearsal • Drink water rather than alcohol before going into the room • Face the group in the room rather than hide from them
'C' (Cognitive): People are waiting for me to screw up	**'C' (Cognitive):** Some people may be waiting for me to screw up, but most won't be

In this chapter, I have discussed helping the client to identify the central mechanism that explains their nominated problem. In doing so, I referred to my work in SSI-CBT (WD). The following chapter will consider how I deal with the central mechanism (in the form of problematic cognitions) that accounts for the client's nominated problem.

25

The session, 6: Dealing with the central mechanism

In this chapter, I will consider how to deal with the central mechanism in the form of problematic cognitions that account for the client's nominated problem. Here, you will wish to use your preferred CBT approach. If you believe these problematic cognitions are best modified, you will use your preferred strategies, aware of the constraints on your time that SSI-CBT imposes. Suppose you think that such cognitions need to be mindfully accepted as a prelude to value-based action. In that case, you will use appropriate metaphors and in-session demonstrations to implement this strategy. Or perhaps you practise a mixed approach and consider that the main issue is when to encourage clients to modify their problematic cognitions and when to encourage them to accept these cognitions mindfully. In what follows, I outline and demonstrate my approach to the issue.

Dealing with the central mechanism (problematic cognitions) in SSI-CBT (WD)

Once the client has understood the connection between their central mechanism in the form of problematic cognitions (in this case, a rigid attitude) and their nominated problem and between their new central mechanism in the form of healthy cognitions (in this case, a flexible attitude) and their goal, the next step is to help them to stand back and examine both sets of cognitions. In SSI-CBT (WD), my task as a therapist is twofold. First, I need to help my client understand why their rigid and extreme attitudes are problematic for

DOI: 10.4324/9781003214557-28

them. Second, I need to help them understand why their alternative flexible and non-extreme attitudes are healthy for them. Here are the steps I tend to take.

1. First, I take both attitudes at once and ask my client questions about the empirical status, the logical status and the pragmatic status of each. I also ask them for their reasons for their answers.

Windy:	First, let me help you to stand back and consider both attitudes so that you can make an informed decision about which one is best for you. OK?
Eugene:	OK.
Windy:	So to remind you, your rigid attitude is, 'I prefer not to have the defect of getting nervous and I prefer that others don't see it and therefore both these things must not happen', and your flexible attitude is, 'I prefer not to have such a defect, and I prefer that others don't see it, but unfortunately that does not mean that both of these things must not happen'. Is that right?
Eugene:	That's correct.
Windy:	Now, which of these attitudes is consistent with reality and which is not consistent with reality?
Eugene:	The rigid attitude is not consistent with reality, while the flexible is.
Windy:	Why?
Eugene:	Well, just because I demand that I don't get nervous and that others don't consider this a defect doesn't mean that these things won't happen. When my attitude does not demand this, it matches reality better.
Windy:	Which attitude is sensible and which isn't?
Eugene:	My rigid attitude is nonsense because it is magical. It implies that I can stop people from

177

> thinking that I have a defect because I demand
> this. My flexible attitude is not magical and,
> therefore, sensible.

Windy: Which attitude will have better results for you
and which will have worse results?

Eugene: As you have helped me see, my rigid attitude will
lead to me being anxious, which won't help me
give good group presentations. But my flexible
attitude will lead me to be concerned, which will
help me improve my group presentation skills.

2. I then ask my client if they have any doubts, reservations
and objections about weakening their rigid attitude and
strengthening their flexible attitude. Finally, I deal with any
misconceptions they may reveal in their response.

Windy: Do you have any doubts, reservations or
objections to weakening your rigid attitude and
strengthening your flexible attitude?

Eugene: Well, if I do this, I will be more likely to give a
group presentation and expose myself to others
seeing me nervous.

Windy: And then they may think you have a defect.

Eugene: Yes.

Windy: And if they did, what would that mean to you?

Eugene: That I am defective.

Windy: As a person?

Eugene: Yes.

Windy: OK. Shall we stand back and consider that idea?

Eugene: OK.

Windy: Do you have any children?

Eugene: No, but I plan to have one or two one day.

Windy: So would you sit your children down and teach
them to regard themselves as defective if they

	reveal their nervousness to others and they think of them as showing a defect?
Eugene:	No, of course not.
Windy:	Why not?
Eugene:	Because I love them.
Windy:	So are you saying that you would privately think of them as defective, but out of love you would teach them that they weren't?
Eugene:	No, I am not saying that.
Windy:	So help me understand?
Eugene:	I would teach them that if they revealed their nervousness to others and these people considered them doing so as a defect, then they weren't defective.
Windy:	What attitude would you encourage them to take towards themselves under these circumstances?
Eugene:	That they were normal human beings who got nervous in public.
Windy:	And would you encourage them to hold this attitude towards themselves if others considered them defective human beings for having a 'defect'?
Eugene:	Yes, I would.
Windy:	Why?
Eugene:	Because it would be true and...Oh, the penny drops...[*Laughs*]...and sensible and helpful for them.
Windy:	You know what I am going to ask you now?
Eugene:	If I would teach my children to regard themselves as normal human beings even if others view themselves as defective for getting nervous, why can't I apply this attitude to myself?
Windy:	Exactly. Why can't you?
Eugene:	I can, and I will.

3. My next step is to encourage my client to see that they will begin to think in problematic ways the next time they encounter their adversity but can respond to this. Thus, their first reaction is to be expected, but it is how they respond to this first response that is important (see Chapter 12).

> *Windy:* I think that it is important that you understand that the next time you consider giving a group presentation, then you may well begin to get anxious because you will start to think in the same rigid way that you have done before. It is important that you don't get discouraged by this. It is a function of habit, and habits can be changed. So when this happens, respond by reminding yourself of your flexible attitude. Is that clear?
>
> *Eugene:* Yes, it is.

4. After I have helped my client to examine their rigid and extreme attitudes, on the one hand, and their flexible and/or non-extreme attitudes, on the other, dealt with any doubts, reservations and objections they have expressed and made the point about the importance of their subsequent response to their first reaction, I ask them to summarise the work we have done so far. I prefer them to do this rather than summarise the work myself because I am mindful that the client will be taking away what they have learned rather than what I have shown them.

> *Windy:* So why don't you summarise what you have learned so far about dealing with your anxiety problem?
>
> *Eugene:* Well, first you showed me that the rigid attitude I held towards having and showing a defect when giving a group presentation explained my anxiety and if I wanted to be concerned but not anxious about doing so, I needed to develop and

> strengthen a flexible attitude towards having and
> showing a defect. You also helped me see that
> I could see myself as a normal human being
> and not a defective one even if others think I am
> defective, and I never thought about this before.
>
> *Windy:* And the point about your initial reaction to
> adversity?
>
> *Eugene:* That it is a matter of habit and that it is important
> to respond to it when it happens.

5. I then suggest to my client that they can use similar strategies in examining their rigid and extreme attitudes, on the one hand, and their flexible and non-extreme attitudes, on the other, when dealing with their problem in different contexts. In this way, they can generalise their learning.

6. My next step is to encourage my client to step back and examine their inferential 'A' if it is clear that it may be distorted. This is usually done after I have helped the client assume that their inferential 'A' is true and to deal with it as above. Sometimes, however, it transpires that the client does not respond well to my strategy of helping them to deal constructively with the adversity. In which case, I will help them to examine the adversity instead. For example, as I have shown in my work with Eugene, I first helped him deal constructively with his inferential 'A' that getting nervous meant he had a defect that he would also reveal to others. Then I did the following:

> *Windy:* So far, we have assumed that getting nervous
> when giving a group presentation is evidence of a
> defect, but let's stand back and look at that. OK?
>
> *Eugene:* OK.
>
> *Windy:* If a very good friend told you that they got ner-
> vous while giving a group presentation, would
> you tell them they had a defect?

Eugene:	No.
Windy:	Would you privately think that they had a defect but wouldn't tell them?
Eugene:	No, I would not think that.
Windy:	So, if you did not think that them showing nervousness proved they had a defect, what would you believe it meant?
Eugene:	That they had an anxiety issue.
Windy:	What's the difference between a defect and an anxiety issue?
Eugene:	An anxiety issue is not a pejorative term, while a defect is.
Windy:	So, if your good friend showed that he was nervous while giving a group presentation, he would have an anxiety issue and not a defect, while if you showed nervousness in the same situation, you would have a defect?
Eugene:	Yes, I see what you mean.
Windy:	You see that you have a choice: to see your nervousness as an anxiety issue or as a defect.
Eugene:	Yes, my first instinct is to see it as a defect...
Windy:	And when you stand back and think of your friend?
Eugene:	Then I can see that I have an anxiety issue and not a defect.
Windy:	What difference would that make to you?
Eugene:	I wouldn't feel so ashamed of getting nervous.
Windy:	So you have two ways of dealing with your shame. First, to be flexible in your attitude about having and showing a defect and, second, to see that getting nervous isn't a defect.
Eugene:	Which is the best approach?
Windy:	My suggestion is that you first develop and rehearse a flexible attitude towards the defect and then question whether it is a defect.

7. Finally, I encourage my client to use mindfulness-based techniques under certain conditions. Thus, when a client has spent some time modifying a problematic cognition, be it a rigid and/or extreme attitude or a distorted inference, that problematic cognition may linger in the person's mind after that work has been done. Rather than encouraging my client to use this continuing presence as a cue to renew modifying that cognition, I suggest that they accept the presence of that thought in their mind without engaging with it or attempting to get rid of it. Then I encourage them to get on with whatever they would be doing if the thought was not in their mind. I see cognitive modification as akin to spending time in a gym. It is time-limited, and the benefit will accrue over time. As with the gym, rest periods are essential.

In this chapter, I discussed the important issue of changing the central mechanism that accounted for the client's problem and used my work as an SSI-CBT practitioner to demonstrate the points discussed. In the next chapter, I will discuss the importance of making an impact in SSI-CBT so that the work you do with the client is meaningful for them.

26

The session, 7: Making an impact

In my view, when working with clients in SSI-CBT, you should avoid working with them in a dry and intellectual manner. Instead, it is important to engage them emotionally. However, it is also important that your clients are not overwhelmed with emotion so that they cannot think. Making an impact on your clients means helping them to engage both 'head' and 'heart' as they address their problems with you.

Here is a list of strategies that may help make the SSI-CBT process more impactful for your clients. Please bear in mind that one well-chosen method is likely to be more helpful than trying overly hard to increase the impact of therapy using several techniques in a short period. In SSI-CBT, here as elsewhere, often 'less is more'.

Find and use something that resonates with your client while helping them

It is difficult to know what will resonate with your client concerning helping them deal with their nominated problem. Here are a few tips, though. First, you need to listen carefully to your client's language in their contacts with you. If they use certain words or phrases frequently, this may indicate that such language is meaningful to them, particularly if it is accompanied by affect. The same applies to any recurrent imagery to which they may refer. Second, observe if your client demonstrates engagement with the language and concepts you use in the sessions. Such engagement may be marked by affect,

DOI: 10.4324/9781003214557-29

an increase in attention, forward leaning and the repetition of language that you may use. Of course, how you use any of this material will vary from client to client. Still, the best way of doing so will be to promote cognitive change, which will be facilitated if the client is emotionally engaged in this process.

Structure your interventions in ways that reflect how your client has been helped and has helped themself in the past

It is important to discover what experiences your client has had in being helped and helping themself both in general and, more specifically, concerning their nominated problem. Then, you can use these helping principles and self-helping principles to facilitate change with respect to this problem.

> Eugene indicated that exposure to threat and bearing discomfort while doing this helped him with a problem earlier in his life. Consequently, I used several opportunities to remind him of his successful application of these principles and helped him to see how he could use them while tackling his nominated problem. In addition, I showed Eugene how he could rehearse his flexible and self-accepting attitudes before giving a group presentation and hold these attitudes in mind while he was in the situation.

Make use of your client's strengths

When you know what strengths your client considers they have, you can refer to these strengths at judicial times in the SSI-CBT process to make their self-change efforts more meaningful and therefore more impactful.

When Eugene expressed a doubt about his capability to apply some of the ideas we discussed in the session, I reminded him that he might surprise himself with determination (his stated strength) concerning what he could achieve. He seemed to resonate with this way of highlighting determination as a response to such doubt.

Refer to your client's role model or to someone who has been helpful in the client's life

Referring to your client's selected role model or someone who has been helpful to them can galvanise your client, particularly when they appear to be flagging. However, what is more important is helping your client keep the person in mind after practising what they have learned in the session.

Eugene selected his paternal grandfather as someone who might be influential in the SSI-CBT process and pointed to a helpful saying that he associated with his grandfather, namely: 'What is very bad now will not seem so bad in the morning.' This phrase nicely encapsulates the non-extreme attitude known as a non-awfulising attitude. I encouraged Eugene to use a version of it, should he encounter people who did regard his nervousness as a defect: 'It might seem awful at the time if people thought that my nervousness was a defect, but it would not seem so bad the next day.' Eugene said that if he imagined his grandfather saying this to him with his arm placed around Eugene's shoulder, this would be particularly impactful, and I encouraged him to do so.

Utilise your client's learning style

The more you can utilise your client's learning, the more likely it is that they will benefit from SSI-CBT, assuming that they relate to the ideas you have helped them develop.

Eugene said that he learned best by giving himself some time to think things through and particularly disliked being rushed. While it may seem that this would pose a particular challenge, given that time is at a premium in SSI-CBT, I encouraged Eugene to take his time at various points in the process. The time he took was, in my opinion, well spent since he appeared to be more involved in the process at the end of each period of reflection. However, he also came up with a few reservations about the usefulness of flexible attitudes that revealed some misconceptions about this concept that I could address. Nevertheless, once Eugene took his time to digest my points, he became more committed to the constructiveness of attitude flexibility.

Utilise the visual medium as well as the verbal medium

CBT is classified correctly as a talking therapy, and as such there is a lot of verbal communication between client and therapist. However, to enhance the impact of SSI-CBT, it is useful sometimes to present visual representations of verbal concepts, especially for those clients whose learning is enhanced by the visual medium. Figures 26.1 and 26.2 present two examples of such visual presentations that I use in SSI-CBT (WD).

In Figure 26.1, I show how I teach the distinctions between flexible and rigid attitudes visually. As shown, both are based on what the person deems important. In a rigid attitude the person holds that

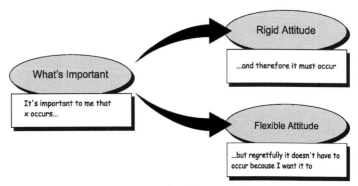

Figure 26.1 Rigid attitude vs flexible attitude

what they deem important must exist, and in a flexible attitude the person acknowledges that they do not have to get what they deem important to them.

In Figure 26.2, I present the 'Big I–Little i' technique, which shows that the 'big I', which represents a person, comprises myriad aspects represented by little 'i's'. It shows that a person cannot be defined by any of their parts.

Refer to your client's core values to promote change

Discovering your client's core values can assist you in helping your client to connect their goals and goal-directed activities to their values. A client will probably strive more persistently towards a goal when a core value underpins it than when it does not.

I discovered that Eugene's stated core value was honesty. I referred to this value initially to create a state of dissonance in Eugene, who, by hiding his 'defect', was not taking an opportunity of being honest with others in the sense of showing them that he was a person who got nervous when giving a group presentation. He could resolve this dissonance either by honestly deciding to show his 'defect' while rehearsing the flexible and self-acceptance attitudes that he constructed or by realising that he was not being true to his core value by deciding not to do this. He decided to take the former path.

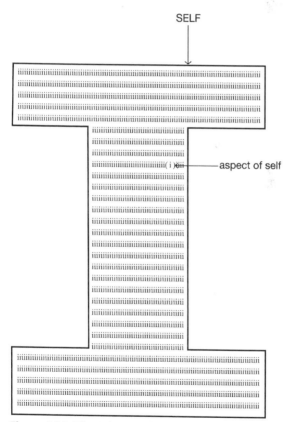

Figure 26.2 The 'Big I–Little i' technique

Use humour judiciously

The use of humour in therapy has attracted various viewpoints amongst practitioners (e.g. Lemma, 2000). My view is that it has the potential to be useful in increasing the impact of SSI-CBT. This is especially the case when:

- The client shows that they have a sense of humour
- The humour is directed affectionately at some aspect of the client, but not at the client themself
- The client can laugh at themself
- The humour has a therapeutic message that can be accurately articulated ideally by both client and therapist
- The client can use that message in the service of their goals

However, humour can be harmful, and it is important that if you use humour, you pay attention to the client's response and seek feedback. It may also be useful to ask the client at the outset whether therapist use of humour would be welcomed.

Consider using self-disclosure

Like therapist humour, therapist self-disclosure can be very useful in increasing the impact of SSI-CBT for some clients, but clients do not universally welcome it. Therefore, if you want to share a personal experience with a therapeutic message for the client, it is probably wise to alert the client to your intention and ask for permission before doing so.

Therapist self-disclosure tends to be therapeutic, therefore, when:

- It is wanted
- It shows that the therapist has had a similar problem but is not ashamed about admitting it to self and others
- It shows the therapist is equal to the client in humanity

- It indicates what the therapist did to deal constructively with their problem, which may be relevant to the client. It thus has a therapeutic point that may be able to be utilised by the client in addressing their nominated problem and working towards their goals

Even if the client has permitted the therapist to share their experience, it is useful to get feedback concerning both its use and what the client has taken from the disclosure.

> Having obtained his permission, I told Eugene how I dealt with my anxiety about speaking in public due to a stammer that I have, since it was similar to his anxiety about giving group presentations. In particular, he found it helpful when I told him that I accepted myself as a fallible human being for revealing what I thought of as a weakness and how doing so helped me address the issue. In addition, he said that it gave what we were discussing more face validity and personal relevance.

Use a range of techniques to increase impact, but construct your own

There are several techniques that you can use to increase impact in SSI-CBT. In using them, I recommend that you rely on your creativity rather than the creativity of others in increasing impact. For example, something may occur to you in your work with a client that may hit the spot that has never been used before and may never be used again. Given the specific context in which the bespoke intervention arose, it is more likely to be impactful than employing 'off the peg' techniques that others have used to be relevant to particular clients. The bespoke rather than 'off the peg' use of imagery, metaphors and stories is particularly important in this regard.

Help your client to develop a brief, memorable and impactful version of their healthy thinking

One of the problems I have had to wrestle with in SSI-CBT (WD) is how to help the client use a flexible and/or non-extreme attitude in the situation in which they need to use it, i.e. when facing an adversity. You will remember that I discussed flexible and non-extreme attitudes in Chapter 4. If you review that material, you will see that both flexible and non-extreme attitudes tend to be wordy. To increase the impact of these attitudes and help clients use them when facing adversities, my practice is to assist them in developing a version of the healthy attitude that reflects its meaning, but that is brief, memorable and meaningful. I encourage clients to note this statement and even use it as a screen saver on their smartphone so that they can refer to it quickly when needed.

I helped Eugene develop the following brief, memorable and impactful version of his healthy attitude: 'A defect proves I'm human, not defective. I don't have to hide it.'

In this chapter, I discussed the importance of impacting the client in the session and outlined several ways of doing this. The following chapter will discuss how to help your client implement their learning from SSI-CBT both inside and outside sessions.

27

The session, 8: Encouraging the client to apply learning inside and outside the session

As in other CBT-based therapy formats, it is important that you help your client to apply what they learn from SSI-CBT, but you only have two shots at doing so. Your first opportunity is when you ask your client to engage in an in-session task, and your second is when you encourage them to think about how they might apply this learning in their life.

Helping the client apply learning inside the session

Suppose you practise CBT, where cognitive modification prominently features when you help your client apply what they have learned so far from the SSI-CBT process in the session. In that case, you are looking for an opportunity to practise their new helpful cognition and act in ways that support its development. In my view, there are three ways of doing this: (1) role-play, (2) two-chair dialogue and (3) imagery. In addition to providing an opportunity to practise new ways of thinking and behaviour, these methods also serve to increase the impact of SSI-CBT on your client (see Chapter 26).

Role-play

There are several ways in which you might employ role-play in SSI-CBT to facilitate client learning. Here are some of the most common:

DOI: 10.4324/9781003214557-30

1. You play a person in your client's life (e.g. a boss), and your client is themself communicating to the other person, having first got into a healthy frame of mind that you have already helped them develop.

2. You play the client, and the client plays the other person in the above scenario. This can be used when the client has found being themself difficult in the role-play. Then, having modelled healthy communication and, if possible, the healthy thinking that underpins such behaviour, you switch roles, and the client can be themself again.

3. You play the unhealthy thinking part of the client, and the client speaks from their healthy thinking part, and the purpose of the resultant dialogue is for the client to strengthen their conviction in their healthy thinking.

4. You play the healthy thinking part of the client, and the client speaks from their unhealthy thinking part. The purpose of the resultant dialogue is for you to demonstrate ways of responding to unhealthy thinking to which the client had struggled to respond when they spoke from their healthy thinking part. Roles are then reversed to enable the client to gain experience in responding effectively to unhealthy thinking.

Two-chair dialogue

In two-chair dialogue, the client switches between chairs in communicating with another person – the client plays both parts – or with another part of themself. Again, the ultimate purpose of such dialogue is for the client to gain experience of acting constructively while rehearsing healthy thinking. I recommend Kellogg's (2015) innovative work on transformational chairwork in this context.

Imagery

In using imagery, you encourage your client to imagine facing an adversity that features in their nominated problem. In doing so, they imagine themself thinking healthily and then acting constructively.

Because, in most cases, when your client faces the adversity, they will first think unhealthily and then respond to such unhealthy thinking with healthy thinking, I recommend that you suggest that your client builds this process into their in-session imagery. Otherwise, they may get discouraged when they find that their first thinking response to the adversity in real life is an unhealthy one.

Suppose you practise CBT where mindful acceptance of cognition predominates rather than its modification. In that case, you will employ various methods to help your client develop their skills in this area (see Harris, 2019).

> I encouraged Eugene to use imagery towards the end of the session in the following way: 'Close your eyes and imagine that you are about to give a group presentation and have begun to feel anxious because you think that you may experience and show your nervousness and think that this means you have and are seen to have a defect. Now remind yourself that "A defect proves I'm human, not defective. Therefore, I don't have to hide it." Hold that attitude in mind as you see yourself give the presentation with due un-anxious concern.'

Helping the client apply learning outside the session

In a sense, the most critical part of the SSI-CBT process is one over which you, as a therapist, have no control. This is where your client chooses whether or not to implement what they have learned in their life when the main part of the process ends.[1] If they choose to do so, you will not have the opportunity to review what they did until the follow-up session held at a time decided upon by the client. This is what delineates SSI-CBT from ongoing CBT. In the latter, your client would be expected to do regular negotiated 'homework' assignments. You would review what they did each week, and the continuity of the execution of such tasks largely determines the outcome of ongoing CBT. In SSI-CBT, while what the client *first* decides to do to implement their learning is important, what perhaps is more important is realising that they need to commit themself to ongoing implementation.

From a cognitive modification perspective, this implementation should ideally reflect the following principles, expressed here directly to the client:

- Use a brief and memorable version of your healthy thinking
- Your behaviour should be consistent with the healthy thinking that you wish to develop
- You should have your healthy thinking in your mind before acting on this thinking
- Practise thinking healthily and acting constructively while facing the adversity listed in your nominated problem
- As you face your adversity, you may find yourself slipping back into your old pattern of unhealthy thinking. This is normal, and respond to it with your healthy thinking when this happens
- You will experience discomfort during this whole process of change. Expect this and bear it. Remind yourself that it is in your long-term interests to do so
- If necessary, rehearse what you plan to think and do in your mind's eye before doing so in real life
- Recognise that you may be tempted to keep yourself safe while facing your adversity. It is best not to act on this urge. If you do so, you won't help yourself in the long term
- Commit yourself to regular practice of your healthy thinking and the behaviour that supports it
- If you keep practising, your feelings will eventually change
- Look for ways of generalising your learning from the adversity listed in your nominated problem to other related adversities

How many of these principles you will want to discuss with your client will depend on what your client wants to achieve and what they can usefully digest. You may want to give your client the above list as a handout with instructions to focus on one principle at a time.

From the perspective of CBT based on mindfulness and acceptance principles, the emphasis will be on helping the client act in value-based ways while acknowledging troublesome cognition and emotion without engaging with them or attempting to eliminate them.

> Eugene resolved to give a group presentation every week while rehearsing the short form of his flexible and self-acceptance attitudes that I discussed in the previous chapter: 'A defect proves I'm human, not defective. I don't have to hide it.' He also agreed to use imagery rehearsal, described in this chapter. Finally, he thought it would also be helpful if he reminded himself that getting nervous is a problem, not a defect, after he had practised thinking healthily about having and being seen to have the so-called defect (see Chapter 25).

In this chapter, I discussed the importance of the client applying their learning both inside and outside the session. In the following chapter, I will consider the importance of ending the session well.

Note

1   There is still, of course, the follow-up session to be held, which I will discuss in Chapter 30.

28

The session, 9: Ending well

After discussing the important issue of how your client will apply what they have learned from the SSI-CBT process to relevant situations in their life, you are coming to the end of the session. It is important to end well so that the client leaves with a sense of hope and having had their morale restored.

You have to do three main tasks to ensure that the client leaves on a high note: have them summarise the work, specify a helpful takeaway from the session, and tie up any loose ends.

Have the client summarise the session and provide a takeaway

While it would be perfectly possible for you to provide a summary of the session, having your client provide the summary enables them to draw actively on their understanding of the process and yields important information concerning what they are likely to take away from SSI-CBT. Once the client has provided the summary, you may prompt the client with any points they have not covered and you think it is important to get covered. Here is how Eugene summarised the process:

> I came to you because I considered getting nervous while giving group presentations meant that I had and was showing a defect. You helped me see that my rigid attitude towards this

DOI: 10.4324/9781003214557-31

was the problem, and you helped me develop the idea that a defect proves I'm human and not defective, and I don't have to hide it. So thinking this way while I give group presentations will help me solve the problem.

(*On being prompted concerning what healthy negative emotion he would feel about having and being seen to have the defect, Eugene responded that he would feel concerned. Also, when asked what resources he could use to achieve his goal, Eugene mentioned 'perseverance' and 'being open about himself', which I regarded as being synonyms for what he said initially, i.e. 'determination' and 'honesty'*).

Dealing with loose ends

In my opinion, your client needs to leave the session with a sense of completeness about the process. Thus, it is useful that you provide an opportunity for the airing of last-minute issues by asking: 'Is there anything we did not cover today that you would like me to know about concerning the problem. Are there any questions you would like to ask me?' In this respect, a question that I particularly favour is this: 'If when you get home, you realise that you wish you could have asked me something or told me something, what might that be?' In dealing with your client's concerns, it is important that you respond to them and check that the client is satisfied with your response. In asking these questions, keep the focus on the problem you discussed with the client. Without that focus, the client might be tempted to raise another issue.

Towards the future

Because it is vital that your client leaves with a sense of hope and commitment about implementing what they have learned, it is important to ask them how they feel about leaving the process at this point. This gives them a second, albeit different, way of raising any unfinished business, as was the case with Eugene (see below). If your client responds with optimism, then it is important to reinforce this. However, you also have another chance to respond to any lingering doubts and reservations they may have about putting into practice the learning they have derived from the process. Here is how I concluded the session with Eugene in this respect.

Windy:	Before we finish, how do you feel about implementing what you have learned here when you give group presentations?
Eugene:	Well, basically, I'm hopeful about it.
Windy:	Sounds like you have a reservation about it too?
Eugene:	I'm not sure how long I have to keep practising before I get the benefit.
Windy:	Yes, I understand your concern, and I wish I could give you a timetable. However, I will say that the more regularly you practise, the quicker you will derive benefits from that practice. Then one day you will realise that you are no longer anxious but still duly concerned about giving group presentations. How does that sound?
Eugene:	Yes, of course, I would like to have a timetable, but what you say makes sense.
Windy:	Good. Any other doubts?
Eugene:	No, I'm looking forward to getting going.
Windy:	I'm pleased about that, and with your determination I'm sure that your hopes will be realised. Now, let's plan a date for our three-month follow-up.
Eugene:	OK.

Accessing further help

You will recall that in Chapter 1 I defined single-session therapy as 'an intentional endeavour between the therapist and the client where the former helps the latter take away what they have come for from the session, but where further help is available if needed'. Thus, you can turn to whether the client needs further help at the end of the session. Again, there are several possibilities here:

1. The client says that they need no further help. Therefore, you can proceed to the follow-up stage.
2. The client says that they are not sure if they want further help. Here you can encourage them to go away and reflect on and digest what they learned, put what they learned into practice and let time pass before making a decision. This process would guide them in specifying a time for follow-up.
3. The client needs further help, and you discuss with them what additional help they need. For example, they may need another single session, a block of sessions, ongoing help or a specialist referral if you or the agency you work with provides the required service.

In this chapter, I discussed the importance of ending the session well. Before discussing follow-up in Chapter 30, I want to discuss a topic that is a feature of SSI-CBT (WD). This involves me making recordings and transcripts of the session and sending them to the client if they wish to have these resources.

29

After the session: Reflection, the recording and the transcript

As you will have gathered, there is a lot to get through in the session. This can usually be accomplished in the 50-minute hour, although if you run over that time, that is perfectly fine. However, given the current pace of life, when the client leaves your office, they may be bombarded with several different things competing for their attention. This is particularly the case if they turn on their mobile phone or tablet as soon as they leave you. Therefore, my view is that it is important that your client gives themself some time to reflect on the session they have had with you, particularly on what they have learned and how they are going to implement what they have learned.

For this reason, I suggest to clients that they refrain from re-entering their busy world too quickly and spend about 30 minutes by themselves reflecting on the session, what they have learned, and how they are going to put such learning into practice. Some may wish to reflect in writing and others in thought. One of my SSI-CBT (WD) clients said they would make a drawing during their reflection period. How they reflect is not as important as that they do so.

The recording and transcript in SSI-CBT (WD): aids to reflection

One of the features of my approach to SSI-CBT, which I have referred to throughout this book as SSI-CBT (WD), is that I will make a digital recording of the session with the client's permission which I will send them soon after the session finishes. Then, I will

DOI: 10.4324/9781003214557-32

have the session transcribed by a professional transcriber and, once received, I will send the client the transcript. While the former is part of what I charge for single-session work, the latter involves an additional cost since I have to pay the professional transcriber that I use for this purpose.

These resources aid the client's reflection process after the session and remind the client of what they have learned. Sometimes, they enable the client to focus on aspects of the process that seemed more critical on review than they did at the time. In particular, both contain accurate references to the summary that the client provided themself. In addition, some clients have said at follow-up that the transcript, in particular, allowed them to copy their summary verbatim, which they carried around with them for later review.

Given the vagaries of human memory, both the recording and the transcript provide an accurate reminder of what was covered in the session and are valuable in this respect. Different clients value these media differently. Some value both, while others value one over the other, partly dependent on their learning style. Clients who like the written word value the transcript, while others who learn better by listening will listen to the recording on an MP3 player, smartphone or tablet. Clients who don't like listening to the sound of their own voice definitely prefer the transcript. For these reasons, I provide them with the opportunity to have both the recording and the transcript. Occasionally, a client does not want me to record the session, and I do respect this wish.

While it is not a part of the process, occasionally a client may wish to comment on some aspect of the recording or transcript. I will acknowledge this and respond, if necessary, but I will not engage in an ongoing dialogue. If necessary, I will explain this and tell the client that I look forward to speaking with them at the follow-up session, which needs to be organised at the end of the session. I discuss this in the next and final chapter.

30

Follow-up and evaluation

The follow-up session is the final phase of the SSI-CBT process. I usually organise this at a time selected by my client after the session, but agencies may have set rules about this which you will have to follow.

Follow-up: for, against or client choice

Not everybody in the single-session therapy community is in favour of carrying out a follow-up session. Given this, let me begin by presenting the arguments for and against follow-up and presenting a third option that involves giving the client a choice on the matter, which I favour.

Arguments in favour of follow-up

First, let me present the arguments in favour of carrying out follow-up sessions.

1. Follow-up provides an opportunity for your client to give feedback on what they have done in the time between the session and the follow-up session. Some argue that your client is more likely to do the work they need to do to achieve their goal if they are expected to provide such feedback.
2. Knowing that a feedback session is scheduled offers your client a sense of care and connection with you as a therapist.

DOI: 10.4324/9781003214557-33

3. A follow-up session provides the client with an (additional) opportunity to request more help if needed.
4. Follow-up enables you and any service in which you work to carry out outcome evaluation (i.e. how the client has done). If you do this, you will have to give some thought to how you will measure outcome and what forms, if any, you are going to use.

> Suppose you are in a service that depends on funding. That may influence your views on this point since, increasingly, funding will only be given to new enterprises if the collection of outcome data is built into the enterprise. In addition, once a new enterprise has been established, continued funding will only be forthcoming if SSI-CBT can be shown to be effective in that treatment setting.

5. Follow-up provides service evaluation data (what the client thought of the help provided), and such data will help your organisation improve the service offered.

Arguments against follow-up

Now, let me present the arguments against carrying out follow-up sessions.

1. Single-session therapy is what it is – a single session. Providing a follow-up session isn't single-session therapy. After all, the argument goes, in walk-in services follow-up is not a part of what is on offer.
2. As noted above, follow-up creates in the client's mind an ongoing connection with the therapist. Rather than this being a positive feature, it serves to dilute the 'this is it' impact of the single session.

3. Not having an opportunity to contact you as a therapist at follow-up gives your client complete control. It is like a trapeze artist working without a net.

Client choice

A third approach involves giving the client a choice concerning whether to be involved in follow-up. I favour this approach because it actualises the 'client decides' principle, a prominent feature of single-session thinking. Having said that, if you work in an agency that mandates follow-up, you will not be able to give your client a choice in the matter.

Formal follow-up vs informal check-in

If you decide to incorporate follow-up into your SSI-CBT approach, you need to decide whether to carry out a formal follow-up or an informal check-in. Formal follow-up entails a detailed and precise evaluation of outcome and the service. It should be agreed at the end of the session and a date put in the diary. Informal check-in is a looser, more general update on the client's progress.

Follow-up in SSI-CBT (WD)

Let me outline my approach to follow-up.[1] At the end of the session, I make a definite appointment to have a follow-up phone or Zoom call, which lasts about 20 minutes. My practice is to schedule the session at a date stipulated by my client after the session. I recommend that they choose a time for the follow-up when they consider that the changes they have made in their life have become stable. I stress to the client the importance of being able to talk without interruption and give their full attention to the call.

I have developed a protocol for the follow-up phone session, which can be found in Table 30.1.

Table 30.1 Follow-up telephone or online evaluation protocol

1. Check that the client has the time to talk now (i.e. approximately 20 minutes)? Are they able and willing to talk freely, privately and in confidence?

2. Read to the client their original statement of the problem, issue, obstacle or complaint. Ask: 'Do you recall that?' 'Is that accurate?'

3. Using a 5-point scale, how would you rate how things are now with respect to the issue?

   (1)   (2)   (3)   (4)   (5)

   Much worse   About the same   Much improved

4. What do you think made the change (for better or worse) possible? If conditions are the same, ask 'What makes it stay the same?'

5. If people around you give you the feedback that you have changed, how do they think you have changed?

6. Besides the specific issue of...[state the problem], have there been other areas that have changed (for better or worse)? If so, what?

7. Now please let me ask you a few questions about the therapy that you received. What do you recall from that session?

8. What do you recall that was particularly helpful or unhelpful?

9. Have you been able to make use of the session recording and/or transcript? If so, how?

10. Using a 5-point scale, how satisfied are you with the therapy that you received?

(1)   (2)   (3)   (4)   (5)

Very dissatisfied   Moderately satisfied   Extremely satisfied

11. Did you find single-session therapy to be sufficient? If not, would you wish to resume therapy? Would you wish to change therapist?

12. If you had any recommendations for improvement in the service that you received, what would they be?

13. Is there anything else I have not specifically asked you that you would like me to know?

Thank the client for their time and participation. Remind them that they can contact you again if they require additional services.

Follow-up: Eugene

In Table 30.2, I provide my notes on my telephone follow-up session with Eugene.

Table 30.2 Follow-up telephone call with Eugene

1. Check that the client has the time to talk now (i.e. approximately 20 minutes)? Are they able and willing to talk freely, privately and in confidence?

   Eugene confirmed that he had the time to talk and could talk freely

2. Read to the client their original statement of the problem, issue, obstacle or complaint. Ask: 'Do you recall that?' 'Is that accurate?'

   I reviewed with Eugene that he came for help with anxiety about giving group presentations

3. Using a 5-point scale, how would you rate how things are now with respect to the issue?

(1)   (2)   (3)   (4)   (5)

Much worse   About the same   Much improved

Eugene provided a score of '5'

4. What do you think made the change (for better or worse) possible? If conditions are the same, ask 'What makes it stay the same?'

Eugene said that he was able to put into practice what he learned in the SSI-CBT process and gave weekly group presentations instead of avoiding them

5. If people around you give you the feedback that you have changed, how do they think you have changed?

Eugene mentioned that his colleagues have remarked that he seems much more relaxed at work than he used to and more specifically that his group presentations are more informal and more humorous, qualities that his colleagues said they valued

6. Besides the specific issue of...[state the problem], have there been other areas that have changed (for better or worse)? If so, what?

Eugene said that he feels more relaxed at work and has more time for his friends than he used to. He attributed both of these things to dealing effectively with his group presentation anxiety problem

7. Now please let me ask you a few questions about the therapy that you received. What do you recall from that session?

Eugene recalled quite a lot since he made full use of the recording and the transcript, particularly the latter. He said what he remembered most was developing the short, memorable version of his healthy attitude

8. What do you recall that was particularly helpful or unhelpful?

Eugene said that what was most helpful was using the short memorable version of his healthy attitude before every group presentation. The least helpful aspect was not being able to have contact with me before the agreed follow-up. Eugene said that he wanted to share his successes with me, but felt that he couldn't

9. Have you been able to make use of the session recording and/or transcript? If so, how?

> *Eugene said that he made much use of both the recording and the transcript, particularly the latter. He had highlighted bits of the session that he found particularly helpful and referred to it whenever he thought he needed to. He did say that as he made progress, he made less use of both the recording and the transcript*

10. Using a 5-point scale, how satisfied are you with the therapy that you received?

(1)   (2)   (3)   (4)   (5)

Very dissatisfied   Moderately satisfied   Extremely satisfied

> *Eugene provided a score of '5'*

11. Did you find single-session therapy to be sufficient? If not, would you wish to resume therapy? Would you wish to change therapist?

> *Eugene said that the SSI-CBT was sufficient*

12. If you had any recommendations for improvement in the service that you received, what would they be?

> *No recommendations*

13. Is there anything else I have not specifically asked you that you would like me to know?

> *Eugene remarked that it would be useful to have this service provided on the National Health Service*

Thank the client for their time and participation. Remind them that they can contact you again if they require additional services.

This brings us to the end of the book. I hope you have enjoyed reading it and that you may be inspired to develop your SSI-CBT practice. If so, and you wish to tell me of your experiences, please email me on my website: windy@windydryden.com

Note

1   It should be borne in mind that my SSI-CBT (WD) practice is one that is conducted in an independent practice setting. I have no pressure on me to provide anyone with formal outcome data.

References

Armstrong, C. (2015). *The Therapeutic 'Aha!': 10 Strategies for Getting Your Clients Unstuck*. New York: W.W. Norton.

Barkham, M., Connell, J., Stiles, W. B., Miles, J. N. V., Margison, F., Evans, C., and Mellor-Clark, J. (2006). Dose–effect relations and responsive regulation of treatment duration: The good enough level. *Journal of Consulting and Clinical Psychology*, *74*, 160–167.

Barrett, M. S., Chua, W. J., Crits-Christoph, P., Connolly Gibbons, M. B., and Thompson, D. (2008). Early withdrawal from mental health treatment: Implications for psychotherapy practice. *Psychotherapy: Theory, Research, Practice, Training*, *45*, 247–267.

Batten, S. V. (2011). *Essentials of Acceptance and Commitment Therapy*. London: Sage.

Beck, A. T. (1976). *Cognitive Therapy and the Emotional Disorders*. New York: International Universities Press.

Bohart, A. C., and Wade, A. G. (2013). The client in psychotherapy. In M. J. Lambert (Ed.), *Bergin and Garfield's Handbook of Psychotherapy and Behavior Change*, 6th edn (pp. 219–257). Hoboken, NJ: John Wiley & Sons, Inc.

Bordin, E. S. (1979). The generalizability of the psychoanalytic concept of the working alliance. *Psychotherapy: Theory, Research and Practice*, *16*, 252–260.

Buckingham, M., and Clifton, D. (2014). *Now, Discover Your Strengths*. London: Simon & Schuster.

Burry, P. J. (2008). *Living with 'the Gloria Films': A Daughter's Story.* Ross-on-Wye: PCCS Books.

Cahill, J., Barkham, M., Hardy, G., Rees, A., Shapiro, D. A., Stiles, W. B., and Macaskill, N. (2003). Outcomes of patients completing and not completing cognitive therapy for depression. *British Journal of Clinical Psychology, 42*, 133–143.

Carey, T. A., Tai, S. J., and Stiles, W. B. (2013). Effective and efficient: Using patient-led appointment scheduling in routine mental health practice in remote Australia. *Professional Psychology: Research and Practice, 44*, 405–414.

Cooper, M., and McLeod, J. (2011). *Pluralistic Counselling and Psychotherapy.* London: Sage.

Davis III, T. E., Ollendick, T. H., and Öst, L.-G. (Eds.). (2012). *Intensive One-Session Treatment of Specific Phobias.* New York: Springer.

Dryden, W. (2009). *Understanding Emotional Problems: The REBT Perspective.* Hove, East Sussex: Routledge.

Dryden, W. (2011). *Counselling in a Nutshell*, 2nd edn. London: Sage.

Dryden, W. (2017). *Single-Session Integrated CBT (SSI-CBT): Distinctive Features.* Abingdon, Oxon: Routledge.

Dryden, W. (2018). *Very Brief Therapeutic Conversations.* Abingdon, Oxon: Routledge.

Dryden, W. (2019). *REBT in India: Very Brief Therapy for Problems of Daily Living.* Abingdon, Oxon: Routledge.

Dryden, W. (2021a). *Windy Dryden Live!* London: Rationality Publications.

Dryden, W. (2021b). *Seven Principles of Doing Live Therapy Demonstrations.* London: Rationality Publications.

Dryden, W. (2021c). *Seven Principles of Single-Session Therapy.* London: Rationality Publications.

Dryden, W. (2021d). *Single-Session Therapy @ Onlinevents.* Sheffield: Onlinevents Publications.

Dryden, W. (2021e). *Rational Emotive Behaviour Therapy: Distinctive Features*, 3rd edn. Abingdon, Oxon: Routledge.

Dryden, W. (2022a). *Reason to Change: A Rational Emotive Behaviour Therapy Workbook.* Abingdon, Oxon: Routledge.

Dryden, W. (2022b). *Understanding Emotional Problems and Their Healthy Alternatives*, 2nd edn. Abingdon, Oxon: Routledge.

Duncan, B. L., Miller, S. D., and Sparks, J. A. (2004). *The Heroic Client: A Revolutionary Way to Improve Effectiveness through Client Directed, Outcome Informed Therapy.* San Francisco, CA: Jossey-Bass.

Eccles, J. S., and Wigfield, A. (2002). Motivational beliefs, values and goals. *Annual Review of Psychology*, *53*, 109–132.

Ellis, A. (1959). Requisite conditions for basic personality change. *Journal of Consulting Psychology*, *23*, 538–540.

Ellis, A. (1963). Toward a more precise definition of 'emotional' and 'intellectual' insight. *Psychological Reports*, *13*, 125–126.

Ellis, A. (2001). *Feeling Better, Getting Better, Staying Better: Profound Self-Help Therapy for Your Emotions.* Atascadero, CA: Impact Publishers.

Ellis, A., and Joffe, D. (2002). A study of volunteer clients who experienced live sessions of rational emotive behavior therapy in front of a public audience. *Journal of Rational-Emotive & Cognitive-Behavior Therapy*, *20*, 151–158.

Harris, R. (2019). *ACT Made Simple: An Easy-to-Read Primer on Acceptance and Commitment Therapy*, 2nd edn. Oakland, CA: New Harbinger Publications.

Hayes, S. C. (2004). Acceptance and commitment therapy: Relational frame theory, and the third wave of behavioural and cognitive therapies. *Behavior Therapy*, *35*, 639–665.

Hoyt, M. F. (2011). Foreword. In A. Slive and M. Bobele (Eds.), *When One Hour is All You Have: Effective Therapy for Walk-in Clients* (pp. xix–xv). Phoenix, AZ: Zeig, Tucker, & Theisen.

Hoyt, M. F., Bobele, M., Slive, A., Young, J., and Talmon, M. (Eds.). (2018). *Single-Session Therapy by Walk-in or Appointment: Administrative, Clinical, and Supervisory Aspects of One-at-a-Time Services.* New York: Routledge.

Hoyt, M. F., and Talmon, M. (Eds.). (2014a). *Capturing the Moment: Single Session Therapy and Walk-in Services.* Bethel, CT: Crown House Publishing Ltd.

Hoyt, M. F., and Talmon, M. (2014b). What the research literature says: An annotated bibliography. In M. F. Hoyt and M. Talmon (Eds.), *Capturing the Moment: Single Session Therapy and Walk-in Services* (pp. 487–516). Bethel, CT: Crown House Publishing Ltd.

Hoyt, M. F., Talmon, M., and Rosenbaum, R. (1990). *Sixty Attempts for Planned Single-Session Therapy*. Unpublished paper.

Hoyt, M. F., Young, J., and Rycroft, P. (2020). Single session thinking 2020. *Australian and New Zealand Journal of Family Therapy*, *41*, *218–230.*

Hoyt, M. F., Young, J., and Rycroft, P. (2021). (Eds.). *Single Session Thinking and Practice in Global, Cultural and Familial Contexts: Expanding Applications*. New York: Routledge.

Jenkins, P. (2020). Single-session formulation: An alternative to the waiting list. *University and College Counselling*, *8*(4), 20–25.

Jones-Smith, E. (2014). *Strengths-Based Therapy: Connecting Theory, Practice and Skills*. Thousand Oaks, CA: Sage Publications.

Keller, G., and Papasan, J. (2012). *The One Thing: The Surprisingly Simple Truth Behind Extraordinary Results*. Austin, TX: Bard Press.

Kellogg, S. (2015). *Transformational Chairwork: Using Psychotherapeutic Dialogues in Clinical Practice*. Lanham, MD: Rowman & Littlefield.

Kelly, G. A. (1955). *The Psychology of Personal Constructs. Volumes 1 and 2*. New York: W. W. Norton.

Lazarus, A. A. (1993). Tailoring the therapeutic relationship, or being an authentic chameleon. *Psychotherapy: Theory, Research, Practice, Training*, *30*, 404–407.

Lemma, A. (2000). *Humour on the Couch: Exploring Humour in Psychotherapy and in Everyday Life*. London: Whurr.

Lewin, K. (1951). *Field Theory in Social Science: Selected Theoretical Papers* (D. Cartwright, Ed.). New York: Harper & Row.

Maluccio, A. N. (1979). *Learning from Clients: Interpersonal Helping as Viewed by Clients and Social Workers*. New York: Free Press.

Miller, W. R., and C'de Baca, J. (2001). *Quantum Change: When Epiphanies and Sudden Insights Transform Ordinary Lives*. New York: Guilford.

Padesky, C. A., and Mooney, K. A. (2012). Strengths-based cognitive-behavioral therapy: A four-step model to build resilience. *Clinical Psychology and Psychotherapy*, *19*, 283–290.

Pashler, H., McDaniel, M., Rohrer, D., and Bjork, R. (2008). Learning styles: Concepts and evidence. *Psychological Science in the Public Interest*, *9*, 105–119.

Persons, J. B., Burns, D. D., and Perloff, J. M. (1988). Predictors of dropout and outcome in cognitive therapy for depression in a private practice setting. *Cognitive Therapy and Research*, *12*, 557–575.

Ratner, H., George, E., and Iveson, C. (2012). *Solution Focused Brief Therapy: 100 Key Points and Techniques*. Hove, East Sussex: Routledge.

Reinecke, A., Waldenmaier, L., Cooper, M. J., and Harmer, C. J. (2013). Changes in automatic threat processing precede and predict clinical changes with exposure-based cognitive-behavior therapy for panic disorder. *Biological Psychiatry*, *73*, 1064–1070.

Rogers, C. R. (1957). The necessary and sufficient conditions of therapeutic personality change. *Journal of Consulting Psychology*, *21*, 95–103.

Rosenthal, R., and Jacobson, L. (1968). *Pygmalion in the Classroom*. New York: Holt, Rinehart & Winston.

Safran, J. D., Segal, Z. V., Vallis, T. M., Shaw, B. F., and Samstag, L. W. (1993). Assessing patient suitability for short-term cognitive therapy with an interpersonal focus. *Cognitive Therapy and Research*, *17*, 23–38.

Salkovskis, P. M., Clark, D. M., Hackmann, A., Wells, A., and Gelder, M. G. (1999). An experimental investigation of the role of safety-seeking behaviours in the maintenance of panic disorder with agoraphobia. *Behaviour Research and Therapy*, *37*, 559–574.

Simon, G. E., Imel, Z. E., Ludman, E. J., and Steinfeld, B. J. (2012). Is dropout after a first psychotherapy visit always a bad outcome? *Psychiatric Services*, *63*(7), 705–707.

Slive, A., and Bobele, M. (Eds.). (2011). *When One Hour is All You Have: Effective Therapy for Walk-in Clients*. Phoenix, AZ: Zeig, Tucker & Theisen.

Slive, A., McElheran, N., and Lawson, A. (2008). How brief does it get? Walk-in single session therapy. *Journal of Systemic Therapies*, *27*, 5–22.

Talmon, M. (1990). *Single Session Therapy: Maximizing the Effect of the First (and Often Only) Therapeutic Encounter*. San Francisco, CA: Jossey-Bass.

Wegner, D. M. (1989). *White Bears and Other Unwanted Thoughts: Suppression, Obsession, and the Psychology of Mental Control*. New York: Viking/Penguin.

Weir, S., Wills, M., Young, J., and Perlesz, A. (2008). *The Implementation of Single-Session Work in Community Health*. Brunswick, Victoria, Australia: The Bouverie Centre, La Trobe University.

Westmacott, R., Hunsley, J., Best, M., Rumstein-McKean, O., and Schindlera, D. (2010). Client and therapist views of contextual factors related to termination from psychotherapy: A comparison between unilateral and mutual terminators. *Psychotherapy Research*, *20*, 423–435.

Young, J. (2018). SST: the misunderstood gift that keeps on giving. In M. F. Hoyt, M. Bobele, A. Slive, J. Young, and M. Talmon (Eds.), *Single-Session Therapy by Walk-in or Appointment: Administrative, Clinical, and Supervisory Aspects of One-at-a-Time Services* (pp. 40–58). New York: Routledge.

Zvolensky, M. J., Bernstein, A., and Vujanovic, A. A. (Eds.). (2011). *Distress Tolerance: Theory, Research, and Clinical Applications*. New York: Guilford.

Index

ABC framework: assessment 73–5; case formulation 75–7; central mechanism 169–74; focus 65–6, 70; nominated problem 147–54
Acceptance and Commitment Therapy (ACT) 74
active-directive style 31, 112
additional sessions 33, 201
adversities 42, 48; avoidance 39; central mechanism 181–2; confronting 46–8; goal-setting obstacles 161–3; healthy responses 158–60; identifying 150–1; inferences 47–8; meta-disturbance 46–7; stuck with 46; unhealthy negative emotions 43–5; unhealthy reaction 46; see also reaction responses
anger 44–5
anxiety 43
applying learning 193, 197; imagery 194–5; outside the session 195–7; role-play 193–4; two-chair dialogue 194
approach 23
assessment 73–5, 113–14, 157
attendance 1–2, 5–6, 54–6

attitudes see flexible and non-extreme attitudes; rigid and extreme attitudes
authentic chameleon 32, 103–4
avoidance 39, 87–8

Barkham, M. 55–6
Barrett, M.S. 55
basic assumptions 14–18
Beck, A.T. 4, 42, 74
beginning immediately 22–3
beginning the session 136, 139; help focus 138; with pre-session questionnaire 136–7; problem-focus 138; session goal 138; session purpose 137
behavioural responses 148–9, 159
Best, M. 55
best practice see good practice
Bohart, A.C 55
bonds 30; authentic chameleon 32; core conditions 31; therapeutic style 31
Bordin, E. 30
build on past attempts 16, 117, 185

Cahill, J. 55
case formulation 23, 75–7, 102

C'de Baca, J. 53, 97–8

central mechanism 78–83, 169–70, 176, 183; attitude examination 177–8; client summary 180–1; doubts, reservations and objections 178–9; generalising learning 181; identifying 170–5; inferential adversity 181–2; mindfulness 183; reaction response 180

change: committed reason 51–2; costs of 52; expecting 17; focus 143; knowledge 51; other people 161–2; rapid 50–3

characteristics *see* client characteristics; therapist characteristics

Chua, W.J. 55

client characteristics 95, 101; active engagement 96; activities 100; focus 97; humour 101; implementation 98; metaphors/ aphorisms/stories/imagery 99–100; openness 96; readiness 95; realistic 97–8; specific and general 99

client engagement 184–5

client perspective 54–7

client preferences 26–7, 34, 83, 127–8

client preparation 117–18

client reflection 118, 135, 202–3

client summary 121, 180–1, 198–9

client understanding 119–20

client variables 90, 94; helpful people 91; learning style 93, 117, 187; occasion of self-help 91–2, 185; past problem attempts 16, 117, 185; principles 92; role models 92–3, 186; strengths 17, 25–6, 90–1, 116, 185–6; values 26, 91, 115, 188–9

client-centred approach 17, 24–5, 206

cognitive-behavioural factors 38–40; cognitive responses 149, 159; *see also* ABC framework; central mechanism; reaction responses

cognitive-behavioural therapy (CBT) 2–3, 37; assessment 74–5; conventional clinical mindset 20–1, 23–5, 28; waves 37–8

committed reason to change 51–2

complex problems 18

components 32–4

confronting issues 39

Connell, J. 56

Connolly Gibbons, M. 55

consent 115–16

consultation model 15–16

core conditions 31

Crits-Christoph, P. 55

delivery mode 33

demonstrations 2, 4–5

demonstrative influences 3–5

depression 43

digital voice recording (DVR) 5, 202–3

discomfort tolerance 41

doubts, reservations or objections (DROs) 120, 178–9, 200

drop-in centres *see* walk-in services

dropout 1–2, 55–6

early termination 55–6

Ellis, A. 3–4, 50–2

emotional impact 120–1, 184, 192; bespoke engagement 184–5; creativity 191; humour 190; learning style 187; past successes 185; personal attitude statement 192; role models 186; strengths 185–6; therapist self-disclosure 190–1; values 188–9; visual medium 187–9

emotional problems 43–5, 148, 160, 162; healthy responses 159–60

ending session 33, 121–2, 198, 201; check client's feelings 199–200; client summary 198–9; further help 201; loose ends 199

envy 45

Epictetus 169

Evans, C. 56

exploring an issue 13–14

expressing feelings 13–14

external resources 26, 93–4

extra-therapy variables 15

first contact 32, 123, 127–30

flexible and non-extreme attitudes 38–9, 80–2; central mechanism 172–4, 177, 180–1; client's personal statement 192

focus 27, 112–13, 140–2, 145–6; changing 143; interruption 143–5; problem-focus 64–6, 138, 142–3; solutions 71; *see also* nominated problem; problem-related goal; session goal

follow-up session 33, 117–18, 122, 125–6, 204, 206; evaluation protocol 206–8; example call 208–10; informal check-in 206, 206; reasons against 205, 206; reasons for 204–5

Friday Night Workshops 4–5

further help 33, 201

future-oriented 14–15

generalisation 99, 106, 116, 154–5, 167–8, 181

Gloria-Kathy-Richard films 3–4

goal-setting 142–3, 156, 168; central mechanism 170–4, 176; generalisation 167–8; good practice 114–15; nominated problem 163–6; obstacles 161–3; problem-related goal 18, 27, 68–70, 157; response to adversity 158–60; session goal 18, 27, 67, 138, 156–7; working alliance 34–5

good practice 111, 122; active-directive style 112; build on past successes 117; clear and transparent 112; client preparation 117–18; client reflection 118; client summary 121; client understanding 119–20; doubts, reservations or objections (DROs) 120; emotional impact 120–1; engaging quickly 111; explanation and permission 115–16; focus 112–13; follow-up 122; goal-oriented focus 114–15; imminent future example 113–14; learning style 117; loose ends 121–2; making sacrifices 115; one meaningful point 121; questions 118–19; rapport 111; specificity and generalisation 116

guilt 44

Hardy, G. 55

Hayes, S.C. 37

healthy attitudes *see* flexible and non-extreme attitudes

help at the point of need 20–1

help focus 138

Hoyt, M.F. 1–2, 24–5, 55–7

humour 101, 190

Hunsley, J. 55

hurt 44

imagery 194–5
impact *see* emotional impact
implementation 121, 195–7
inferences 47–8, 181–2
influences 3–6
informal check-in 206
initial point of contact *see* first
    contact
interpersonal problems 40, 161–2
interruption 113, 143–5

jealousy 45
Joffe, D. 4
Joffe, E. 4
Jones-Smith, E. 90–1

Kelly, G. 32

Lazarus, A. 4, 32, 103
learning style 93, 117, 187
Lewin, K. 83
live demonstrations 2, 4–5
loose ends 121–2, 199

Macaskill, N. 55
magic question technique 150–1
Maluccio, A.N. 54–5
Margison, F. 56
Meichenbaum, D. 4
Mellor-Clark, J. 56
meta-problems 40, 46–7
Miles, J.N.V. 56
Miller, W.R. 53, 97–8
mindfulness 183, 197
Mooney, K.A. 90

nominated problem 166;
    adversity 150–1; assessment
    73–5, 113–14; case formulation
    75–7; central mechanism
    78–83, 170–6; focus 64–6, 70–1;
    generalising 154–5; goal-setting
    163–6; meta-problem 151–2;

problem-related goal 18, 27,
    68–70, 157; response systems
    148–9; understanding 147–8,
    152–4

one take away 16, 28, 121
One-At-A-Time Therapy (OAATT)
    12
Öst, L.-G. 2–3, 53
overview 11–14, 123–6
Özil, M. 119

pacing 14, 20, 22, 25; *see also*
    focus
Padesky, C.A. 90
panic disorder 3
past client attempts 16, 117, 185
Perl, F. 3
personal domain 42–5
personal influences: demonstrative
    3–5; practice 5–6
personal journey 3–6
phobias 2–3, 50–3
physiological responses 148
pluralism 75
practice influences 5–6
pre-session questionnaire 33,
    117–18, 124, 131–7
preparation *see* client preparation
present-centred 14–15
principles 92
problem assessment 73–5, 113–14,
    157
problem-focus 64–6, 138, 142–3;
    see also nominated problem
problem-related goal 18, 27,
    68–70, 157; *see also* goal-setting
problematic cognitions *see* central
    mechanism
problems: avoidance 39, 87–8;
    cognitions 85–7, 169–70;
    complex problems 18; emotional
    43–5, 148, 159–60, 162;

interpersonal 40, 161–2; meta-problems 40, 46–7; urges 87–9

quantum change 53
questions 118–19; beginning the session 137–9; goal-setting 156–7

rapid change 50–3
Rational Emotive Behaviour Therapy (REBT) 38, 74–5, 79–83
reaction responses 84, 88–9, 148–9, 180; bypassing adversity 162–3; healthy 158–60; problematic cognitions 85–7; problematic urges 87–9; response systems 148–9
recording 5, 202–3
Rees, A. 55
reflection 118, 135, 202–3
rehearsal 3
Reinecke, A. 3
responses see reaction responses
rigid and extreme attitudes 38–9, 80–2; central mechanism 171–2, 174, 176–8, 180–1, 183
risk management 21
Rogers, C. 3, 31
role models 92–3, 186
role-play 193–4
Rosenbaum, R. 1–2
Rumstein-McKean, O. 55

sacrifices 115
safety-seeking behaviour 3
satisfaction 55–6
Schindlera, D. 55
self-disclosure 190–1
self-help occasion 91–2
service choice 24, 127–9
service delivery 33

session goal 18, 27, 67, 138, 156–7; see also goal-setting
shame 44
Shapiro, D.A. 55
single-session mindset 20, 28; approach 23; client preferences 26–7; client-centred 24–5; external resources 26; focus agreement 27; help at the point of need 20–1; internal strengths and values 25–6; one take away 28; pacing 22; PGS principle 27; session as complete whole 24; starting immediately 22; suitability 25; transparency 22–3
single-session therapy (SST) 1; personal journey 3–6; recent history 1–3
single-session thinking see single-session mindset
social problems 40, 161–2
solution 27, 71, 142–3
solution-focused therapy (SFT) 2, 142
specificity 99, 106, 116
Stiles, W.B. 55–6
strengths 17, 25–6, 90–1, 116, 185–6
subsequent responses see reaction responses
suitability 21; assessment 25; current position 61–3; previous position 58–60
summarising 121, 180–1, 198–9
support network see external resources

Talmon, M. 1–2, 5, 55–7
tasks 35
therapeutic alliance see working alliance theory
therapeutic style 31

therapist characteristics 102; authentic chameleon 32, 103–4; collaborative focus 105; flexible and pluralistic 104; metaphors/aphorisms/stories/imagery 106–7, 191; no client relationship 103; quick thinking 104–5; rapid engagement 103; realistic 105–6; specific and general 106; tolerate low client information 102
therapist self-disclosure 190–1
Thompson, D. 55
time use 14, 20, 22, 25; *see also* focus
transcript 5, 202–3
transparency 23, 62–3, 112, 115–16
two-chair dialogue 194

unhealthy negative emotions 43–5, 160, 162
urges *see* problematic urges

values 26, 91, 115, 188–9
views 32; additional sessions 33; cognitive-behavioural conceptualisation 34; understanding components 32–3
visual medium 187–9

Wade, A.G. 55
walk-in services 2, 61–2
Westmacott, R. 55
working alliance theory 30, 35; bonds 30–2; goals 34–5; tasks 35; views 32–4
workshops 4–5

For Product Safety Concerns and Information please contact our EU
representative GPSR@taylorandfrancis.com Taylor & Francis Verlag GmbH,
Kaufingerstraße 24, 80331 München, Germany

Printed and bound by CPI Group (UK) Ltd, Croydon, CR0 4YY
11/04/2025
01844011-0001